Gathering at the Hearth

Gathering AT THE Hearth

STORIES MENNONITES TELL

Edited by John E. Sharp

Herald
Press

Scottdale, Pennsylvania
Waterloo, Ontario

Library of Congress Cataloging-in-Publication Data
Gathering at the hearth : stories Mennonites tell / edited by
    John E. Sharp.
    p. cm.
    Includes bibliographical references.
    ISBN 0-8361-9161-7 (alk. paper)
    1. Mennonites—History. I. Sharp, John E., 1951-
BX8115.G38 2001
289.7'09—dc21   2001016585

⊛ ∞™

    The stories in this volume are edited and adapted from their original
sources, as credited in the last note for each chapter (on pages 219-22), and are
used by permission. Unless otherwise noted, Scripture is from the *New Revised
Standard Version Bible,* copyright 1989 by the Division of Christian Education
of the National Council of the Churches of Christ in the USA, and is used by
permission.
    Photo credits appear on pages 216-8.

GATHERING AT THE HEARTH
Copyright © 2001 by Herald Press, Scottdale, Pa. 15683
    Released simultaneously in Canada by Herald Press,
    Waterloo, Ont. N2L 6H7. All rights reserved
International Standard Book Number: 0-8361-9161-7
Library of Congress Catalog Card Number: 2001016585
Printed in the United States of America
Cover and book design by Merrill R. Miller

10 09 08 07 06 05 04 03 02 01 10 9 8 7 6 5 4 3 2 1

To order or request information, please call 1-800-759-4447 (individuals);
1-800-245-7894 (trade). Website: www.mph.org

To all who gather at the hearth
to share their stories,
holding together history and hope

Contents

Foreword

HOW CAN WE pass on our heritage of faith to the coming generations? We must tell the stories of faith.

The text of an old gospel song says, "I love to tell the story, of unseen things above, of Jesus and his glory, of Jesus and his love." Surely the good news of Christ's love is the story told most often among Mennonites. Every Sunday morning it is rehearsed in song, sermon, and worship ritual in thousands of congregations in North America and around the world.

If the foundational story of Jesus and his love is to have vitality for us in our time, and if that story is to offer hope for our future, we must know how it has been manifested in our own lives. It cannot remain with "unseen things above." The story of Jesus' love must intersect with our daily living.

Each story in *Gathering at the Hearth* is in its own way a fragment of the master narrative of Christ's love. The fragments are sometimes confessional. They gain power by confronting the darkness within.

Lawrence Hart, in a powerful account of his own coming of age as a youthful Cheyenne Peace Chief, confesses his anger at the American grandsons of Indian killers who take pleasure in reenacting the frontier massacres.

Gerhard Lohrenz, a veteran of the Mennonite Self-Defense force in the Russian anarchy after World War I, agonizes over the decision to take up arms.

If we listen rightly to these stories, we will identify with the justifiable rage which arose in the hearts of young men whose communities were violated. Can the power of love and forgiveness overcome the rage within?

Some of these stories are celebrative. They look back

upon heroes of the faith who exercised extraordinary gifts of leadership and servanthood. In our imaginations these folk may seem larger than life, and gifted in ways beyond our own abilities. But in our own age of cynicism and narcissism, we need to celebrate heroes and role models such as David Goerz, institution builder on the Kansas frontier; Harold Bender, brilliant definer of the Anabaptist vision; and the Brunk brothers, evangelists on spiritual frontiers of the 1950s. The stories of such people can support hope that saints will arise among us and achieve great things for the church and world in the future.

This particular set of Mennonites stories has a special denominational purpose. At a time when larger streams of Mennonites tradition are in the process of merging, members of the different traditions need to listen to each other's stories. General Conference Mennonites of the midwest should pay careful attention to Alice Lapp and John Ruth, to hear about how and why Pennsylvania German Mennonites "kept house" in church affairs as they did. And (Old) Mennonites need to listen to Peter Dyck tell how momentous were the sufferings and migrations of the Dutch-Russian Mennonites.

As we embrace each other's stories, and recognize ourselves in the strengths and weaknesses of others we see as different from ourselves, the cause of unity is served.

There have been times when the church of Jesus Christ has been tempted to separate hope from history. A religious tradition that reflects the Bible's witness cannot afford such a split. Our hope for the future must be nourished by confidence that the workings of God's grace in our past foreshadow fresh outpourings of grace in the future. The coming generations will carry the faith tradition to greater heights. If we tell the stories.

—James C. Juhnke
 North Newton, Kansas
 February 4, 2001

Preface

Once you were not a people
but now you are God's people;
once you had not received mercy,
but now you have received mercy.
—1 Peter 2:10

Mission is linked to identity
as identity is linked to memory.

———

IN BIBLICAL TRADITION collective memory shapes the character and values of a people. The people of Israel were instructed to recite the marvelous deeds of their redeeming God. By retelling the formative stories, they would nourish their own memories, as well as teach the generations that would follow them.

Peter told the scattered Christians of Asia Minor to remember that "once you were not a people, but now you are God's people; once you had not received mercy, but now you have received mercy." Reciting the salvation story was vital to the survival and growth of the church. Memory was the key to identity—for the people of Israel and for the Christian church of the first century.

Memory is also the key to our identity as Mennonite Christians of the twenty-first century. We live in a culture of amnesia: our culture dishonors heritage in general and spiritual heritage in particular. If we acknowledge spiritual heritage at all, we often weaken it by making it a minor thread in the fabric of a national or common cultural inheritance.

We also lose our spiritual legacy when we think of it as

an embarrassment or a hindrance to mission and evangelism, and then grasp for another, generic identity. We fail to realize that identity is linked to memory, as mission is linked to identity. Thus, we are in danger of losing the gospel that has been entrusted to us.

Bruce Birch, Old Testament professor at Wesley Theological Seminary, said it this way:

> Memory is oriented to recalling what God has done and how faithful response has been made to God's action. Vision is oriented to anticipating what God is yet doing in the world and to aligning life to serve that action of God's grace. . . . The community of faith stands with one foot rooted in a historic tradition from which it draws its identity as God's covenant people. Its other foot is firmly planted in a future, God's future, toward which it lives in anticipation of the fulfillment of God's desire for love, justice, and wholeness.[1]

Our mission is also hindered when our memory becomes narrowly selective and relevant to only a few insiders. On the other hand, our identity is enriched and our mission is strengthened when we enlarge our collective memory by hearing and incorporating the stories of new church family members of various racial and language groups. On the threshold of a new century and a new millennium, these sisters and brothers are breathing new life into old stories.

What narratives have shaped and nurtured us? What new stories have the power to reshape and transform us? The stories in this volume have been selected because they reveal something about who we are—or who we want to be. They illustrate core values, as well as failures that have characterized us.

Learning each other's stories is especially critical now as we leave familiar and separate identities—as Mennonite Church (MC, formerly called [Old] Mennonites), General

Conference Mennonite Church (GCMC), and Conference of Mennonites in Canada (CMC)—and become a new entity called *Mennonite Church*. Becoming a transformed people as members of Mennonite Church (USA and Canada) is not about drawing the right organizational charts, about boundaries of new district conferences, or even about theological uniformity.

The needed transformation process is about bringing people together in heart and mind. We are brought together when we tell about events that have shaped and molded us. We are bound together when we hear the stories of the people—mostly ordinary people—whom God has used in extraordinary ways. We are transformed when we remember how God has redeemed our failures and our sins and has endowed us with a rich legacy of faith. This remembering helps us to be agents of transformation as this rich legacy is translated into a vibrant and relevant witness.

—*John E. Sharp*
  Director, Historical Committee and Archives
    of the Mennonite Church
  Goshen, Indiana

The inset image shows a Pennsylvania state historical marker reading:

NORTHKILL AMISH

The first organized Amish Mennonite congregation in America. Established by 1740. Disbanded following Indian attack, September 29, 1757, in which a Provincial soldier and three members of the Jacob Hochstetler family were killed near this point.

PENNSYLVANIA HISTORICAL AND MUSEUM COMMISSION

According to family legend, a lingering Indian named Tom Lions notices the family escaping the burning cabin and calls the attackers back. *Tom Lions* is an artistic depiction by Sam B. McCausland, commissioned by Loren Wengerd.

INSET Marking the spot: A Pennsylvania state historical marker.

Amish or Shawnee? The Hochstetlers of Northkill

John E. Sharp

One of the tales told most often among the Amish is the story of the Indian attack on immigrant Jacob Hochstetler's family in 1757. The Hochstetlers were among the settlers in the first Amish settlement along the Northkill Creek, in northcentral Berks County, Pennsylvania. In the midst of the French and Indian War, 1754-63, Indians aligned with the French against the English, crossed the Blue Mountain, and attacked white settlers, including the Hochstetler family. Many Amish and Mennonites trace their genealogy back to three of the Hochstetler children, John, Joseph, or Barbara. The other brother, Christian, has many descendants among the Church of the Brethren.

THE SCHNITZING PARTY was over. The youth of the Northkill Amish settlement had gathered at the Hochstetler home for a frolic, a work party. They had peeled, cored, and sliced apples for drying. The schnitz—dried apple slices—would be used for baking during the winter months. Work projects often became social events, resulting in both productivity and fun.

The party was over. The young people had gone home, and the Hochstetlers had gone to bed. They didn't know it, but it was the last night for this family ritual.

In the predawn hours of September 20, 1757, the Hochstetlers were aroused from sleep by the incessant barking of the dog. Ten-year-old Jacob got up to investigate. When he opened the door, a gunshot shattered the stillness of the night. A musket ball shattered Jacob's leg. In an instant, the family was up. What was this? Had the war come to their front door?

Through the windows the Hochstetlers could see shadowy figures by the bake oven, some distance from the house. They were Indians!

The Delawares (Lenni-Lenapi) and the Shawnees had once lived and hunted in these Pennsylvania hills and valleys. But William Penn had acquired this land in a series of purchases from the Iroquois, who claimed this territory, confirmed by a deed of 1736.[2] Other treaties were made, disputed, and broken as the settlers pushed the Native Americans from their ancestral homes. The Amish had not directly displaced the Indians, but they *were* part of the endless tide of European American settlers that forced the boundaries of the frontier westward. Incited by the French to weaken the British claims on the colonies, Indian bands raided white frontier settlements.

One such band was now stalking the Hochstetler home. What could they do? Eighteen-year-old Joseph and sixteen-year-old Christian grabbed their rifles. They were excellent marksmen. With their shooting skills, they could defend the family and assure their survival. Surely, this crisis required such action.

Father Jacob was of a different mind. He ordered the boys to put their guns away. Guns were for hunting animals, not for shooting human beings. Indians were humans, created and loved by God. Jacob's anxiety for the family's safety was overruled by the deeply ingrained conviction that Jesus'

teaching about loving one's enemies is practical, not just the-
oretical—even in situations like this.

The guns were put away, and the family, now quite vulnerable, waited to see what the stalkers would do. They did
not have long to wait. The Indians set fire to the house, the
barn, and other farm buildings. The besieged family took
refuge in the cellar, where they used freshly pressed apple
cider to fight back flames piercing the floor above them.

Dawn was breaking, and the Indians began to drift away.
Thinking they had survived the traumatic attack, the family
escaped the burning house through a cellar window—and
into the hands of their attackers. They were spotted by an
Indian lingering to pick fruit in the orchard.

Mother Hochstetler, a daughter, and Jacob Junior were
killed and scalped. Jacob, Joseph, and Christian were taken
captive. An older son, John, who lived nearby, was alerted by
the flames. He came upon the scene only to watch helplessly
as the tragic scene unfolded before him.

The captives were taken across the Allegheny Mountains
into Indian territory, where they were separated and adopted into Native tribes. After several years, Jacob escaped his
village, traveling by night and hiding by day. Eventually he
reached a tributary of the Susquehanna River, built a raft,
and floated downstream. Eventually he was spotted and
pulled ashore, exhausted and famished.

When examined by provincial authorities, Jacob gave this
account of his escape:

> I got the liberty for hunting, one morning very soon [I]
> took my gun finding a Bark Canoe on the River wherein
> I crossed it, traveling E[a]st for 6 Days from there I
> arrvd. at the souce of the west Branch [of the
> Susquehanna River], there I march[ed] for 4 Days fur-
> ther till I was sure of it [that it was the Susquahanna],
> there I took several Bloks tying them together till I got a
> flo[a]tt, there I flo[a]tted myself Down the River for five

Days where I did arrive at Shamokin, Living all the time on grass. [I] pass'd in the Whole for 15 Days.[3]

What about Joseph and Christian? Jacob, with the help of more literate friends, petitioned Lieutenant Governor James Hamilton of Pennsylvania to intervene and return his sons. A part of the negotiated settlement at the end of the French and Indian War was the return of prisoners.

This agreement was less than satisfactory since most Native families were reluctant to give up their adopted members. Furthermore, many adoptees did not want to abandon their Native families and tribes. The attachment between "captive" and "captor" was expressed in the speech of a Shawnee chief as he relinquished adoptees:

> *Fathers, we have brought your flesh and blood to you: they have all been united to us by adoption; and though we now deliver them, we will always look upon them as our relations. . . . We have taken as much care of them as if they were our own flesh and blood. . . . We request you will use them tenderly and kindly, which will induce them to live contentedly with you.*[4]

The Shawnee speech did, indeed, express the deep bonds forged between the Amish boys and their Native American families. Joseph was returned under the conditions of the treaty, and Christian apparently came back on his own. But both struggled to adjust to the strange ways of their once-familiar culture, even schnitzing parties.

Slaughter to the tune of "Garry Owen": the infamous massacre of Black Kettle's peaceful village by U.S. troops led by George Armstrong Custer, November 27, 1868.

INSET Lawrence Hart: Blending the peace traditions of Native Americans and of Mennonites.

A Cheyenne Legacy at the Washita River

Lawrence H. Hart

The cultural clash between European Americans and Native Americans on the Great Plains became severe during the 1860s and 1870s. Homesteading pioneers— Mennonites among them—increased the pressure on Native Americans to vacate their ancestral lands. Little did European American Mennonites realize that they shared a deeply held conviction with some Native Americans: nonresistance to violence. Lawrence H. Hart, a former bomber pilot, embodies this conviction from both traditions: he is a Mennonite pastor and a Cheyenne Peace Chief. In this story Hart revisits a painful, violent event in his history and becomes an agent of reconciliation.

"ODAI! (LISTEN)," a Cheyenne woman whispered in the early morning of November 27, 1868. The noises she heard struck fear to her heart. Four years before, she had survived a terrible massacre at Sand Creek in eastern Colorado. Her fear was especially heightened the evening before when Cheyenne Peace Chief Black Kettle—traveling with warriors Little Robe and Spotted Wolf and Arapaho chief Big Mouth—returned from his visit with Colonel William H. Hazen at Fort Cobb. They had gone seeking an assurance of peace and safety.

Surely the colonel would honor Black Kettle's peaceful cooperation. Had the chief not received a peace medal from the hand of Abraham Lincoln, president of the United States? Was he not flying the American flag given him in the nation's capital as a symbol of his peaceful intentions, as well as a white flag of peace? Had he not signed the treaties of 1865 and 1867? Had he not survived the terrible Sand Creek massacre without making any resistance?

Colonel Hazen refused to give them the protection they sought. He told them that the federal government had initiated a winter campaign to punish them for attacks against Kansas settlers. When the chiefs returned to their respective winter camps with the bad news, everyone was alarmed.

Cheyenne men discussed the impending campaign in Black Kettle's lodge. His wife, Medicine Woman Later, was listening. She had survived nine bullet wounds at Sand Creek and wanted the camp moved immediately, but it was midnight and very cold. The men decided to stay one more night by the banks of the Hooxeeohe, the Cheyenne name for the Washita River in Indian Territory, later to become the state of Oklahoma.

As it turned out, Medicine Woman Later's intuition was right. The unsettling noises she heard that night came from eight hundred approaching troops. Lieutenant Colonel George Armstrong Custer led the Seventh U.S. Cavalry to within striking distance, arriving at midnight. At dawn on November 27, with a foot of snow on the ground, the regimental band of the Seventh Cavalry played their marching song, "Garry Owen," signaling the attack.

Terror struck the Cheyenne. The sword-wielding Custer, who himself would one day die by the sword, ordered the attack from four sides. The troops charged through the cluster of fifty-one lodges, shooting right and left. Hearing the noise of the weapons and the screams, Arapaho and Cheyenne warriors from nearby villages came running.

Eventually, Kiowa, Comanche, and Plains Apache warriors joined the fight.

Twenty-two soldiers were killed and thirteen wounded. Custer's troops captured fifty-three Cheyenne Indians, mostly women. They torched Black Kettle's village, including the winter supply of food and clothing, and slaughtered over eight hundred Cheyenne horses. Black Kettle and Medicine Woman Later tried to escape, but they were shot off their horse and fell into the Washita River.

Lieutenant Colonel Custer reported to his superior officer: "After a desperate conflict of several hours, our efforts were crowned with the most complete and gratifying success."[5] He claimed to have killed 108 warriors, when in fact most of the victims were women and children. Furthermore, he was pleased that Black Kettle's scalp was in the possession of one of his Osage guides.[6]

Chief Black Kettle did what weaker men could not do; he refused to fight violence with violence. He had been taught the words of Cheyenne prophet, Sweet Medicine:

> If you see your mother, wife, or children being molested or harmed by anyone, you do not go and seek revenge. Take your pipe. Go, sit and smoke and do nothing, for you are now a Cheyenne chief.

One hundred years later, the town of Cheyenne, Oklahoma, planned a centennial commemoration of the massacre, now called "the last great battle between the Indians and the U.S. Army in Oklahoma."[7] The organizers asked the Native Cheyenne to participate in a reenactment. But how could they celebrate the brutal attack on their peaceful village? Finally, the Cheyenne reluctantly agreed on condition that they be permitted to bury the remains of a Cheyenne child on display in the local museum.

The reenactment began. Local townsfolk and ranchers played the soldiers of the Seventh Calvary. In a mock village of tepees, Cheyenne adults and children portrayed their ancestors. Unknown to the Cheyenne, however, a California group called the Grandsons of the Seventh Cavalry, Grand Army of the Republic, had been asked to join the reenactment.

This group was dressed in authentic Seventh Cavalry uniforms. Marching to the tune "Garry Owen," they rushed the village, shooting blank cartridges from authentic Spencer carbines. For many Cheyenne people watching, especially those whose children were in the mock village, the events became all too real. Deep feelings of hostility erupted.

Nevertheless, the day's schedule continued. The final event was the reburial of a victim's remains on the grounds of the Black Kettle Museum. As the chiefs, including peace chief and Mennonite pastor Lawrence Hart, left the museum carrying a small, custom-made bronze coffin, they began chanting their special burial songs. Snow was falling as it had fallen a hundred years before.

Over their singing, the chiefs suddenly heard the command, "Present arms!" The Grandsons of the Seventh Cavalry were there. Emotions flared. *How dare they salute someone their grandfathers killed?* thought Hart. In the midst of the charged atmosphere, a Cheyenne woman, Lucille Young Bull, took off her beautiful new woolen blanket and quickly draped it over the coffin as the procession went by. As tradition dictated, the blanket would later be given as an honored gift.

After the burial the older and wiser peace chiefs huddled momentarily. Lawrence Hart speculated that the blanket would be presented to one of the Oklahoma dignitaries in the audience. But the older chiefs had a different plan. They asked Hart to give the ceremonial blanket to the captain of the Grandsons of the Seventh Cavalry! How could Hart do this? This man was the enemy! Hart's own great-grandfather, Afraid of Beavers, had barely escaped the attack by hiding in a snowdrift. Hart's nerves and muscles tensed.

In sharp military fashion, the captain came forward, stopped in front of the peace chiefs, and drew his saber to salute. Hart, the young peace chief, instructed the captain to turn around. Returning his saber sharply, he did an about-face. Hart's trembling hands draped the beautiful blanket over the captain's shoulders.

It was an awesome moment. The wise Cheyenne peace chiefs had initiated a reconciliation that resulted in conflict transformation. At this ceremony, the older peace chiefs indelibly impressed onto the younger chief what it meant to follow the instructions of Sweet Medicine, a prophet of the Cheyenne. To end the ceremony of reburial, the Grandsons fired volleys to honor the victim. There was not a dry eye in the audience.

The Grandsons followed the chiefs back to the museum. Then and there, they embraced. Some cried. Some apologized. When Hart greeted the captain of the regiment, the officer took the "Garry Owen" pin from his own uniform and handed it to Hart. "Accept this on behalf of all Cheyenne Indian people," the captain said. "Never again will you people hear 'Garry Owen.'"[8]

Delp meetinghouse near Harleysville, Pennsylvania, built by the "Funkites," followers of Christian Funk.

INSET Petition of thirteen Mennonite ministers to the Provincial Assembly of Pennsylvania, explaining why Mennonites could not go to war. Fraktur by Roma J. Ruth.

Keeping House as We Understand It

John L. Ruth

*Far too often differences of opinion have splintered con-
gregations and conferences. In the story of Christian
Funk (1731-1811) and the Franconia Mennonite
Conference, John Ruth examines the issues and the core
values that divided them. He points to a "central thread"
of the Mennonite story, what he calls "the requirement
of mutual yieldedness." While this "requirement" protected a sense of community, it promoted little sympathy
for individual deviation from that community.*

———

THE AMERICAN COLONIES were at war—actually, in rebellion. They were determined to cut the strings that tied
them to their British mother-nation. The discord spilled over
into the nonresistant Franconia Mennonite Conference in
eastern Pennsylvania, which had a rebellion of sorts on its
own hands.

Bishop Christian Funk was inclined to favor the side of
the American revolutionaries (since he thought they would
probably win), while his co-ministers stood by their original
promise of allegiance to the "ordained" powers of the
English crown. Funk was even rumored to be willing to take
the new oath of allegiance, while other Mennonites were
jailed and had their properties seized for refusing the new

27

Test Oath that would have made them take back their earlier promise.

The difference of opinion, fed by other neighborly irritations, soon escalated into open animosity, primed by charges and countercharges. The forty-seven-year-old bishop was silenced, then excommunicated. The obdurate, traditional bishops of the conference were convinced they could not maintain order with such an abrasive and independent Funk, who was unwilling to submit himself to the counsel of the church.

Several attempts—one nearly thirty years later—to mend the broken relationship failed. Christian Funk and his "Funkite" followers were never reclaimed.

Was Christian Funk historically "right" or not?

His attitude was seen to be a fundamental threat to the essence of the fellowship, less, ultimately, in his political leanings than in his insistence on following his own lights, whether or not the brotherhood consented. Undoubtedly he was smarter than most, if not all, of his fellow members. Certainly his opponents were merciless and exaggerated in their gossipy criticism. Surely resentment over his self-assertive manner became uncharitable anger.

But "keeping house" in the community of Christ, or "maintaining the right fellowship," which reflected the humility of Christ, was almost the original theme—the basic identity—of this spiritual family that had such difficulty with Christian Funk. When we are considering this topic, we are as close as we can get to the central thread of our story. The requirement of mutual yieldedness, considered by the majority to be a primary feature of their spiritual heritage, could not be suspended when convenient.

Funk himself had some grounds for his charge that the bishops did not use the literal procedure of Matthew 18, which was to deal with an erring brother personally before involving other members. This order, claimed Christian, had been violated in his case, and in that consisted a great wrong.

The main community, on the other hand, was concerned more with symbolic attitude than technicalities of procedure. Its leaders held to the authority of the assembled body to discern and declare that one of its members was out of order and out of fellowship. Without this prerogative, the old deeply felt brotherhood would have had to change something of its essence.

When an individual, however superior in insight, could challenge the authority of the church to define what reconciliation would require, one would have another dynamic than had been worked out two-and-a-half centuries earlier. When the Swiss-South German Anabaptist fellowship had first covenanted into a church, it had spoken of the concept of the "rule of Christ," an "order" that depended on mutual recognition of the church's authority and submission to it. This had become a recognizable tradition, and the special "feel" of it was still predominant in the central district of the "Skippack" Mennonites.

Nearly three-quarters of the members of five congregations polled felt that Christian Funk could be reinstated only after publicly recognizing the authority of the church to call him to account. This requirement, which he flatly rejected, shows where the center of gravity lay in the community. It was not even superseded by the "authority" of the ministers. Eventually, Mennonites would allow more room for individualist initiative. A newer model of democratic procedure would supervene the older idea of mutual resignation. But that too would not come about without strong resistance and an even greater schism.[9]

Refugees of the Civil War looking for safer territory.

INSET Susanna Heatwole Brunk, a stalwart woman of courage in the face of danger and misfortune.

Escaping the Confederacy

John E. Sharp

During the Civil War, Mennonites and other conscientious objectors in the South were forced to serve as combatants or noncombatants in the Confederate Army, pay a fine, or go to prison. Henry G. Brunk and Susanna Heatwole were married in Virginia in 1859, just before the Civil War broke out. Rueben J. Heatwole, born in 1847, was Susanna's younger brother. The events they experienced called for uncommon courage, both during the war and in their later migration to the Kansas Prairies.

———

AFTER THE CIVIL War broke out, Henry Brunk and Rueben Heatwole were with a group of seventy-two young men who tried to escape on horseback, through the mountains to the north, to avoid serving in the Confederate Army. It was 1862. Eventually two Confederate soldiers captured them and took them back to the Shenandoah Valley of Virginia. At Staunton, the Confederate cavalry confiscated their horses. From there, they were sent by train to the Libby Prison in Richmond.

Most of the men chose noncombatant service over imprisonment or duty as soldiers. When released from prison after several months, Henry was assigned to haul hay from the barns of Shenandoah Valley farmers to feed the cavalry horses. But Henry was uneasy—he was still helping the war effort. His conscience prompted him to act.

While Henry was waiting his turn to get a load of hay from yet another farmer's barn, he slipped off through the orchards and woods to his home. For two-and-a-half years, he was a fugitive, hiding in the attics of his Mennonite neighbors—a different attic each night.

Henry had a close call one evening as he was making his way to the next attic. While on the road, he met John Albert Ayray, a soldier recruited from the local community, who was sent to find Henry. Ayray knew Henry well but this time did not recognize him. The soldier asked who in the neighborhood could tell him where Henry G. Brunk could be found. The fugitive, tongue in cheek, answered that a farmer who lived one-half mile west could likely tell Ayray about as much as anyone—which was nothing at all!

Henry was not among the mourners at the cemetery when his little two-and-one-half-year-old son, Johnny, was buried. The father watched from a distance, then hurried away out of sight while the hymn was being sung and the grave was being filled. Confederate scouts were present and watching, but they did not see Henry. Susanna grieved alone.

Brothers-in-law Henry Brunk and Rueben Heatwole were among the seventeen young men who met one midnight at Weaver's Church, west of Harrisonburg. Fifteen were seventeen-year-olds, and two—Henry Brunk and Dave Frank—were older men, army deserters. If captured, they would surely be shot.

Rueben later wrote, "If we could get over safely to the north, we could have good wages as farmhands and need not be soldiers, Yankees, or Rebels." Hired guides led them over the first ridges, but then the guides turned back and the fugitives were on their own. Heatwole later remembered,

We were soon ascending the [next] mountain with courage, even if the soldiers' campfires in the valley were in sight, and behold, in a short distance was a soldier and a picket to guard the camps, having his gun

and sword. When we saw his little fire, . . . we turned'
down the mountain in haste. Brunk and I were behind,
so he could stand on his tiptoes [and] look over the tops
of the brush to see the soldiers who were peeping at us
from behind trees. At the foot of the mountain, we all
lay down quietly, and Frank saw a man, and I, boylike,
wanted to see him too, and then told him it was no
man. If Brunk would say so, I would prove it to him. I
went and brought him a whip from a stump that was
the height and the size of a man. Then very soon he saw
a man with a broad-rimmed hat on. I brought the
"hat," which was only a large piece of bark on top of a
stump like the other one.[10]

After that they thought they saw a cavalry encampment
and made a wide detour. Their food was soon gone, and they
walked miles without water. That night they "nestled down
into a large sinkhole half full of leaves and slept well until
sunrise, regardless of snakes or lizards that might have been
in the leaves."

The band of seventeen chose the tall, capable Henry
Brunk as their leader. He

moved on slowly, and we did not run ahead as we had
done the day before. Looking at his open-faced watch
and the sun, he could find our way. . . . Soon we came
to the house of a widow, who gave us some loaves of
bread. Then in the mountain brush, we quietly ate a fine
breakfast and dinner combined of only dry bread.[11]

The widow told them she hoped her slaves would not find
out they were headed north for fear that they would leave
her to join them.

As they continued their journey, they spotted the "soldiers' tents" they had seen the day before. The "tents"
turned out to be only peach trees in full blossom. The "sol-

diers" were farmers pruning the fruit trees, and the "cavalry horses" were only the farmers' mounts grazing on orchard grass. Before long, however, they met two real soldiers, who demanded that the travelers show their weapons. The men produced New Testaments and pocketknives. Since they were now in West Virginia, and their "weapons" appeared harmless, the men were allowed to proceed.

Later in the day, as they rested under some shade trees, a man with a pistol in hand suddenly appeared. He told them that if he had not first seen the three Negroes in their group, some of the white men would have been shot. (Apparently the widow's slaves had joined them.)

At Clarksburg, West Virginia, they promised allegiance to the Union. Then they walked to Newcreek, Williamsport, and on to Hagerstown, Maryland. Most of the men found employment on farms. Henry Brunk went to work, mending shoes and harnesses. He sent a message to Susanna, asking her to meet him in Maryland.

Susanna packed a spring wagon and started north with baby Sarah, born during Henry's absence, and her sister, Margaret Rodgers. Margaret's husband, Charles Rodgers, had found work on a farm near Hagerstown. Susanna followed the path of the armies, going northward as the Confederates pushed the Union army back.

Confederate soldiers noticed her "sassy steed" and seized him. But Susanna refused to let go of the lines, even when they unhitched her horse from the wagon. Only the warning cry of "Yanks!" turned the attention of the soldiers away from Susanna's fine horse. As they ran, they ordered Susanna to follow. With "sanctified spunkiness" she retorted, "I'll do no such thing!" The women hitched up the horse again and continued their journey northward.

Susanna entered Hagerstown, praying for guidance as she looked for some sign of Henry. How would she find him? Strangely, her horse suddenly stopped in the middle of the street and refused to move. Then she saw Henry through a storefront window, repairing shoes. As a granddaughter later told the story, "Their eyes met, and soon they were together with conflicting emotions of joy and tears. Together they thanked God for the marvelous way he had led them."[12]

The Confederate Army came to Hagerstown three times, and each time the farmers asked the hired men from the south to drive their horses and wagons to safety across the Mason-Dixon Line into Pennsylvania. Rueben Heatwole was "two and one-half miles from Chambersburg when the Rebel soldiers burned the city."

Fearful of Confederate advances, Heatwole and the Rodgers and Brunk families left Hagerstown and traveled by train to Geneseo, Illinois. After eight years and five more children, the Brunk family moved by covered wagon to Marion Center, Kansas. Reuben Heatwole had preceded them and staked claims for himself and the Brunks. He looked forward to "many happy days" with the Brunks.

When the family arrived on the Kansas plains on October 13, 1873, Henry and the six children were sick with typhoid fever. Henry unhitched his horses and crawled under a rude shelter to rest, never to rise again. Eight days later, the once robust Henry was dead at the age of thirty-seven.

By Christmas, Susanna gave birth to Henry Jr., but five-year-old Fannie and eleven-year-old Sarah had also died of typhoid. Before Easter 1874, Henry Jr. had also died. Stalwart thirty-four-year-old Susanna was now a lonely mother with four young children, out on the wild prairie.

Today one can see the four gravestones, still alone in a Kansas field. On Henry Jr.'s gravestone is engraved, "Budded on earth to bloom in heaven." Susanna Heatwole Brunk surely prayed that all her children could bloom awhile on earth before they bloomed in heaven.

Indeed, the four remaining children did bloom and flourish. Among them was George R. Brunk I, who eventually moved to his parents' native Virginia. From there, he became a strong conservative voice in the Mennonite Church.

A monument to a pioneer and his people: Bethel College
Administration Building.

INSET David Goerz, a man of many gifts and many dreams.

David Goerz, Russian Mennonite Pioneer

D. C. Wedel

*In the 1870s, some 18,000 Russian Mennonites settled
on the prairies of the United States and Canada. They
left Russia when the exemption from military service for
young men was withdrawn. They brought a vision for
missions, publications, and education. David Goerz
(1849-1914) was interested in all those ventures and
more. He was a pioneer, not only on the prairies of
Kansas, but also in the General Conference
Mennonite Church.*

June 28, 1849, when David Goerz was born, was a day
that brought joy and happiness to Heinrich and Agnetha
Goerz and a few relatives in the village of Neubereslav near
Berdjansk, Russia. The full significance of this event is still
dawning upon the thousands of people influenced by this
gifted man.

Already during his youth, David Goerz displayed qualities
that led his mother to wish he might become either a minister
or a teacher. It was not long until he distinguished himself as
an outstanding student at the Orloff Vereinschule at
Molotschna. While in school, he earned money to pay some
of his expenses. His teacher taught him the art of surveying,
which he later used extensively on the Bethel College campus.

His proficiency in his study and work program led to an office position with the large Cornies estate. His work was done so well that he was given additional responsibilities.

At the age of eighteen, Goerz began his teaching career in Berdjansk. His eighteenth year was important also because it marked the year of his baptism, which he described as a "wonderful experience." He gave private instructions to the children of Cornelius Janzen at Berdjansk. Berdjansk not only gave him the opportunity to exercise his teaching ability; there he also met Helene Riesen, who later became his wife. They were married on June 29, 1870. Then followed the exciting events that led to the immigration to America.

The Great Migration

The migration to America was preceded by a steady correspondence with his friend Bernhard Warkentin, who had arrived in America on June 5, 1872. In those letters Warkentin told of his experience in meeting leading Mennonites already in America, railroad and land agents, and representatives of the government. He described the prairie states and what could be expected by those who might want to settle there.

David Goerz would copy these letters, often spending most of the night making the copies. He made his copies available to those who were thinking seriously of migrating from the various villages. He also kept his friend in America well informed of the impression his letters made.

In one of these letters, Goerz revealed that Berdjansk, where he, Elder L. Sudermann, and C. Jansen lived, was the nucleus of the migration movement. In a letter dated January 28, 1873, he wrote that Sudermann had been elected a delegate to investigate the conditions in America. He also informed his friend that the neighboring colony, Bergthal, had five hundred families who wanted to go to America.

David and Helene Goerz decided to go to America with a group of Crimean Mennonites, but they were detained because of difficulties in obtaining their passports. They arrived in November 1873 and proceeded to Summerfield, Illinois, where David taught in a Mennonite school and began his little paper, *Zur Heimat.* In 1875, the Goerz family with a group of Summerfield Mennonites settled at Halstead, Kansas. There he continued serving as editor of *Zur Heimat* and was the manager of the Western Publishing House.

When the immigration tide brought many poor people who could not pay for their passage, a relief agency was organized bearing the name "The Mennonite Board of Guardians." David Goerz served as an agent and secretary of this board for sixteen years. He was helpful in seeing immigrants through customs, arranging railroad transportation for them, helping them in their exchange of money, and seeing them located in their new western homes.

Goerz believed in cooperation and organized the first Mennonite Teachers Conference in Kansas in 1877. The Teachers Conference adopted a resolution to call a meeting of the Kansas [Mennonite] Conference, which in 1892 became the Western District Conference. This action was possible because the ministers had been invited to the Teachers Conference, which met in the home of Heinrich Richert, Alexanderwohl, Kansas.

For years Goerz was either secretary or chairman of this church conference. He likewise served as a trustee of the conference from 1887 until his health began to fail in 1910. The constitution of the Western District Conference adopted in 1896 was largely his work. When a committee of three was formed to submit a plan to the conference for carrying on home and foreign mission work, David Goerz was again in the midst of that work. In 1880 he organized the Mennonite Mutual Fire Insurance Company to protect the early pioneers exposed to devastating prairie fires.

Publication and Missions

When in 1875 the Goerz family followed the stream of Mennonite immigration to the West, he transferred his little paper, *Zur Heimat*, from Summerfield to Halstead, Kansas. He continued its publication for six years. *Zur Heimat* was produced by the Western Publishing Company; W. M. Ewert, B. Warkentin, David Goerz, Peter Wiebe, and John Lehman were directors.

In 1881 the German publication of the Eastern District Conference *Der Mennonitische Friedensbote*, and *Zur Heimat* were merged. The new conference paper was called *Christlicher Bundesbote*, published by the General Conference Mennonite Church.

David Goerz was one of those who, having found the "pearl of great price," was also ready to share it. He early developed an interest both in home and foreign missions. In 1890 he read a paper on home missions before the General Conference; it was published in 1892.

In 1900 Goertz made a trip to India to distribute eight thousand bushels of donated grain among the starving natives and to investigate the possibilities of establishing foreign mission work. He found a suitable location around Champa, where the mission to the lepers was later established by P. A. Penner.

Bethel College

David Goerz was also involved in the founding of the Halstead Seminary, which later became Bethel College. The Halstead Seminary was founded in the fall of 1883 as a school to train teachers.

At times the support of the Halstead Seminary was uncertain because congregations belonging to the Kansas Conference failed to raise the budget. Goerz dreamed of collecting an endowment fund to make the school self-supporting. While struggling with this problem of the expansion of the seminary, an offer came that completely surprised the educators. An organization called "The Newton College Association" had been competing with the town of Winfield, Kansas, to have a Methodist college located at Newton. Winfield had won the race, and Newton then invited Mennonites to establish a college there.

A special session of the Kansas Conference of the General Conference Mennonite Church was called for April 27, 1887, to consider the offer. When no decision could be reached, another proposal was submitted: If the conference would not accept the Newton offer, would it permit the formation of a society that might accept the offer and build a college? The conference accepted this idea.

A corporation was formed and a charter drawn up, naming the college "Bethel." The incorporators appointed a board of trustees: John J. Krehbiel, Bernhard Warkentin, David Goerz, Heinrich Ewert, D. C. Ruth, Abraham Quiring, C. R. Mclain, J. M. Ragsdale, and A. B. Gilbert.

The cornerstone of the Bethel College administration building was laid on October 12, 1888. Even before the building was completed, it was evident that the college would need more buildings. This need was partly met when the buildings of the Halstead Seminary were purchased. The best of them were moved to the Bethel College campus.

Goerz worked at the problem of finding ways and means for student housing. When the need for a dormitory for young women became acute, he urged his friend Peter Jansen to write Andrew Carnegie and express this need. Somewhat dubious about the outcome of the venture, Peter Jansen wrote and soon had a reply that held little promise for a gift. Jansen wanted to give up, but not Goerz. He insisted on further negotiations and told Jansen what he should write and how he should make this urgent need clear to Carnegie. Goerz's persistence through Jansen brought a gift of $10,000 for the dormitory, now know as Carnegie Hall.

Bethel College opened its doors in the fall of 1893 with C. H. Wedel as the first president. David Goerz served as the first business manager. He wanted Bethel to be the best school possible and wanted to attract the best faculty.

Goerz wanted the Bethel campus to be beautiful. The monument to this desire is seen in the home he built on the campus—Goerz Hall. In planning for the beauty of the campus, he made frequent use of his knowledge of surveying, which he had learned in Russia.

David Goerz continued to serve Bethel until 1910, when ill health compelled him to relinquish this work. Bethel was, however, always in his thoughts. As he neared death, he called his son Rudolph to his side and said, "You will do for our Bethel what you can, won't you?" After Rudolph reassured his father that he would do what he could, Goerz smiled and breathed his last.

Hospital Work

David Goerz was also a pioneer in deaconess work. Others may have entertained the thought that there was a place in serving God's kingdom for women; Goerz was the first to express this interest and act upon it. In 1890 he read a paper before the General Conference Mennonite Church convening in South Dakota, emphasizing the importance of deaconess work. His paper was based on a wide reading of books on the topic. The more he read, the more he became interested.

Three years later, when the General Conference met in Ohio, the delegates instructed the Board of Home Missions to make this work its concern. In 1900 Frieda Kaufman presented herself as a deaconess candidate to David Goerz.

Goerz was ready to leave for India but made a vow that if he would return in safety, he would do all he could to establish the deaconess work. Meanwhile, he made arrangements at Bethel College to have Sister Frieda begin preparatory studies.

The next step in the development of deaconess work was the action taken by directors who arranged to have candidates continue their education and training in the Deaconess Hospital in Cincinnati, Ohio. The Board of Directors of Bethel College next formed the Bethel Deaconess Home and Hospital Society. The state charter was granted on March 30, 1903.

Two years later, the society bought a property in Newton. In 1907 the building contract for a hospital was signed, and on June 11, 1908, the building was dedicated. On the same day the first three deaconesses—Sister Frieda Kaufman, Sister Catherine Voth, and Sister Ida Epp—were ordained and installed into service.

As Minister

David Goerz was also gifted as a minister and touched many lives. His sermons are described as models of clear thought and logical arrangement. Congregations to be visited by Goerz waited for his coming with anticipation, not only for the content of the sermon, but also for its effective presentation. While his sermons were primarily expository, he always insisted on a practical Christianity without minimizing the deeper spiritual life. They were the product of careful preparation and much prayer.

As a pastor, Goerz possessed a deeply sympathetic nature. He could enter into the discouragement, disappointment, and sorrow of people and give comfort to the most dejected. With the tenderness of feeling he possessed, it was not always easy to be obedient to the demands his logical thinking made upon him. Yet when his feelings threatened to swerve him from his duty, he refused to follow feelings alone.

Goerz had many opportunities to serve people in a spiritual ministry. The Halstead congregation called him and ordained him in 1878. In 1897 he became pastor of the Bethel College Mennonite Church. His ministry to the young people is especially remembered by those whom he served.

As a lover of music, Goerz enjoyed the chorales in the *Gesangbuch mit Noten*. He took a prominent part in the publication of the *Kleiner Liederschatz*. At least one song in the *Gesangbuch mit Noten* is published under his name. He often led both local and community choirs.

Goerz loved books. He read extensively. Because he was blessed with a retentive memory, he could use much of what he read. He was well read in literature and in theology, although biography and the sciences came in for their share of time. He had an extensive library and contributed much to the founding of the Bethel College library.

Although Goerz's travels were mostly for business purposes, he thoroughly enjoyed them. His travels and writing activity made him one of the most widely known and respected men in the General Conference Mennonite Church. In a sense, David Goerz was a lonely man, a lone worker. His ideas, his dreams, and his aspirations were so far ahead of his people that there were often only a few who understood what he was trying to do. But he had patience to wait and to work until others could catch something of his vision and his dreams.

The word *defeat* had no place in his vocabulary. He had clarity of thought that could bring order out of chaos. When complicated questions came before the conference, his keen analysis would point in the right direction. Much of his success may be due to the fact that he worked with restless energy, often spending many hours of the night working because the day had been too short.

The contributions of David Goerz were the ripened fruit of a rich life. He was a Mennonite pioneer, a business executive, a teacher, an editor, a surveyor, a relief worker, a minister and elder, a merchant, a family man, a community leader, but above everything else, a man of God.[13]

Conferring: a gathering of the Central Conference and the Middle District of the General Conference Mennonite Church, Danvers, Illinois, 1898.

INSET Joseph Stuckey, the father of a conference.

Father Stuckey and the Central Conference

John E. Sharp

*"Father" Joseph Stuckey (1826-1902) of the North
Danvers Church in central Illinois is remembered as a
strong, nurturing father figure. His patience with erring
members of his congregation is recalled by some as a
good model. Most of his fellow Amish ministers saw it
as a failure to exercise proper correction, which compromised the integrity of the church's faith and witness.
Consequently, they parted fellowship with Stuckey. The
congregations under his oversight became known as the
Stuckey Amish, who later joined with the Middle District
of the General Conference Mennonite Church to form
the Central District Conference.*

––––––

AMISH BISHOP JACOB Stuckey of central Illinois made his
living by tilling the rich Illinois prairie soil. And he followed his calling to become the spiritual shepherd of his
Amish congregation.

Born in the Alsace region of France in 1826, he migrated
with his parents to Butler County, Ohio, in 1830. As an
adult, he moved to McLean County, Illinois, which was
being settled by Amish from Pennsylvania, Switzerland, and
Alsace. Stuckey joined the "Pennsylvania" Amish congregation of Rock Creek, east of Peoria. He was ordained minister in 1860 and bishop four years later.

His congregations knew him as the rather conservative "Father Stuckey." Others counted him as the founder of the more liberal Stuckey Amish, who parted ways with the conference of Amish ministers in 1872.

Was he both conservative and liberal? Yes. He was conservative theologically, as were most Amish leaders. But he was considered liberal in his reluctance to apply the expected discipline of erring members—at least in one case. This case has defined him and the Stuckey Amish, who stood by their leader during the controversy.

It's true that, like some other congregations of the day, the Stuckey Amish were showing signs of moderating the old order. They had abandoned the pattern of worshiping in members' homes and had built a meetinghouse. Hooks and eyes on clothing gradually gave way to buttons and collars. Other traditional symbols of plainness, separation, and humility became less pronounced. Congregations in other settlements were making similar changes; eventually they were called Amish Mennonites.

There was something else that troubled Amish leaders, even the changing Amish Mennonites. It was a poem written by a member of Stuckey's congregation, the elderly schoolteacher-poet, Joseph Yoder. The poem's title was "Die frohe Botschaft" (The Good News). The poem's message was a "correction" to commonly accepted teachings of salvation and eternal punishment.

The poem began innocently enough with a concept central to all Christian teaching:

> This is a faithful saying
> And worthy of all acceptance,
> That Jesus Christ came into the world
> To save sinners.

Already in the second verse, the divergent theology becomes apparent:

Such teachings
As we frequently hear
Of eternal torment in hell
Cannot possibly be the truth;
They deny God's goodness
And make his spirit harsh.

In verses 15 and 16, Joseph Yoder becomes strident in his opinion about conventional teaching and its teachers:

It is not at all reasonable [to believe]
That in the future the torment of hell
Should last forever.
Only insanity can so delude us
As to believe or hear
What God's word does not teach.
[This idea] is pure fable,
A heathen suggestion;
Lack of understanding honors only
The darkness in the corner;
Sectarian presumption
Builds up hatred and quarreling.

The schoolteacher-poet's universalism reaches full expression in verse 26, the final stanza:

Love flows forth from God
And works its way into the whole of creation,
Makes everything like unto itself,
Until the whole earth
Shall become one universe,
A heavenly kingdom of peace.[14]

The poem came to the attention of the 1870, 1871, and 1872 Amish Mennonite Ministers' Conferences, where it was read to the assembly. Alarmed, the chairman and the assistant chairman addressed the assembly "very earnestly and powerfully" about the false doctrine it contained. They warned that the poem could lead the young people astray and make the godless feel comfortable in their sin. Such a member should be admonished; if unrepentant, he should be removed from membership.

The following Sunday, Joseph Stuckey met Yoder at the door of the meetinghouse with the verse in hand and asked whether he had written the poem. When Yoder said he had, the bishop said, "You can't be a member."[15] But Stuckey was reluctant to remove the eighty-five-year-old man from the fellowship, even though he disagreed with his theology. Stuckey "set the poet back" from communion but did not excommunicate him.

Stuckey's colleagues in the conference took his reluctance to excommunicate the errant member as a weakness, as tolerating sin. They believed that the theological integrity of the church was being compromised and that to continue fellowship with Stuckey was to be unequally yoked with an unbeliever. Hence, two leaders from the East visited the Amish congregations in Illinois to take counsel regarding the difficulty. Believing there was support for the action, the eastern ministers told Stuckey that since he regarded Yoder as a brother, they could no longer count *Stuckey* as a brother.

Joseph Stuckey continued his leadership roles in central Illinois, overseeing several congregations, in addition to North Danvers, his home congregation. As he organized new congregations and ordained new ministers, his influence grew. By the time of his death in 1902, he had ordained eighteen bishops, performed over two hundred marriages, baptized over thirteen hundred new believers, and preached countless sermons.

Just before the turn of the century, in 1899, the Stuckey Amish congregations organized as the Central (Illinois) Conference of Mennonites. After the organizational meeting, the seventy-four-year-old bishop commented, "The child is born. Name and nourish it, but be careful how you do it."[16] Was he remembering the authority of the conference once used to discipline him twenty-seven years earlier?

The Central Conference and "Father Stuckey's" influence expanded to include other congregations beyond the state boundaries. Congregations who found themselves at odds in theology and practice with their own conferences sought refuge under Stuckey's nurturing hand.

Meanwhile the Stuckey Amish developed cooperative relationships with the Middle District of the General Conference Mennonite Church in missions and education. The Middle District suggested merger, but the Central Conference was reluctant.

In 1945 the Central Conference applied to be admitted as a district of the General Conference Mennonite Church. When the application was submitted to the conference assembly, the Stuckey Amish experienced culture shock. A Central Conference minister, unaccustomed to the formal procedures of the General Conference, was dumfounded to hear a brother pronounced "out of order!"[17]

Furthermore, the smaller, closely knit Central Conference was afraid of being swallowed up by the larger, more formal Middle District. The merger discussions stalled. After much more conversation and many more official actions, the two finally merged in 1957. The most convincing overture came when the larger Middle District unexpectedly asked to join the smaller Central Conference![18]

The Stuckey Amish were then united with a larger Mennonite denomination. When the current transformation process—the joining of the Mennonite Church and General Conference Mennonite Church—becomes official, the Stuckey Amish will commune once again with the Amish Mennonites, who have since the separation of 1872, become part of the Mennonite Church.

Surely, "Father Stuckey" would rejoice!

Seeking the Promised Land in Canada: Schellenberg family from Schonwiese, leaving Russia on what was called "the second Immigration Train," 1923.

INSET David Toews, a Moses for his people.

David and the Promised Land

D. J. Schellenberg and Peter Dyck

*David Toews (1870-1947) became the central figure in
the immigration of twenty thousand Russian Mennonite
refugees to Canada, 1923-30. He knew what it was like
to be a migrant. Born in the Trakt settlement in Russia,
he and his parents migrated to Turkestan, and then
joined the ill-fated trek to Asia. Incredibly, the Toews
family, with nineteen other families, retraced their steps
back through Russia, on to Germany, and eventually to
Kansas. David Toews later moved to Saskatchewan,
Canada, where he became a teacher, pastor, elder, and
administrator. The story of his work as chairman of the
Canadian Board of Colonization is a story of remarkable
patience, persistence, and faith.*

MOSES LED THE people of Israel out of slavery in Egypt,
toward the Promised Land. Klaas Epp led a group of
Mennonites on a devastating journey to a promised land in
Asia, to await the second coming of Christ. David Toews,
influenced by both these journeys, became a modern Moses
for twenty thousand Mennonites from Russia who migrated
to Canada in the 1920s.

The Toews ancestral home was Weisshof near
Tiegenhagen, in West Prussia (now Poland). Economic hard-

ships in the middle of the nineteenth century, as well as political pressures threatening the core value of peacemaking,
prompted Mennonites to seek homes elsewhere. A group
migrated to Russia and in 1853 founded the Trakt settlement
near the Volga River, in the province of Samara. Jacob and
Maria Wiebe Toews were among these settlers. A year later,
on February 9, 1870, David Toews was born to Jacob and
Maria in Lysanderhöh, Russia.

The new settlement at Trakt faced serious issues. From
within, differences concerning the second coming of Christ
threatened to divide them. From without, universal military
service, which the Mennonites wanted to avoid by going to
Russia, became a threat. An apparent solution was presented: General Kaufmann, the governor of Tashkent, Turkestan,
offered Mennonites complete exemption from military service if they would settle in his territories in Asia.

In response to this invitation, many Mennonite families
again set out, on a journey to a promised land. It was a dangerous trek. They faced the burning heat and shifting sands
of the desert, the daunting height of the mountains, and the
fearful depth of canyons. Accidents caused many delays, as
did the occasional collapse of oxen pulling the heavily loaded
wagons. Typhoid, cholera, and smallpox plagued the travelers. Those who died were buried along the way.

In Russia the pilgrims traveled by way of Saratov and
Orenburg. In Asia they followed the military road of Syr-
Darya through Kasalinsk, Perowsk, Kaplanbeck, and the
beautiful, fertile plateau of Tashkent. There they heard
unsettling news: Russian Czar Alexander II had died, and so
had Governor Kaufmann. What was to become of them
now?

The government of Tashkent offered them land several
hundred miles east of Tashkent and promised them an
acceptable form of alternative service. Those who accepted
the offer founded the Aulie-Ata settlement, which later
became a well-established colony.

Others continued further east under the leadership of Klaas Epp and founded a village, Ak Metchet, in the domain of the khan of Khiva in October 1882. There they suffered theft and murder at the hands of Turkish tribesmen. The dream of the expected paradise vanished. Klaas Epp, who predicted the time and place of the Lord's return, became more and more fanatical.

Some of the Khiva settlers realized that there would be no rest or prosperity in this barren land; they wrote letters to relatives in America. As a result, a group of about twenty families packed up again. This time they headed west, back the way they had come, to the Volga River and through Russia, then further west, through Germany and over the Atlantic Ocean to America. After more than four years of wandering since they first left Prussia, the beleaguered immigrants arrived in Newton, Kansas, in the fall of 1884. Among them was David Toews, fourteen years old.

Already the young Toews had seen more of the world than most teenagers dream about. He had traveled by foot or in a wagon over three continents—Europe, Asia, and North America. He had no idea how this prepared him for his most important contribution to his people.

David worked on the farm of Bernhard Regier, and then attended the Halstead (Kansas) Seminary, where he studied under H. H. Ewert and C. H. Wedel. He taught school at Elbing and Newton, Kansas, and was baptized into the Mennonite church in Newton in 1888. Five years later, his former teacher, H. H. Ewert, invited him to Gretna, Manitoba, to teach school.

Toews completed his formal education at Wesley College and Normal School, in Winnipeg. In 1898 he received a call to teach in Saskatchewan. The Mennonite settlements northwest of Rosthern, at Tiefengrund, were recently settled by immigrants from the Vistula Delta area in Prussia. A common origin united teacher and students.

The youthful teacher was truly a man of the people, living with them and for them. Characterized as cheerful and optimistic, he was loved and respected by young and old. Alongside teaching, he also farmed. In 1900 he married Margarete Friesen, from Tiefengrund, Saskatchewan. David and Margarete became parents of eight children, one son and seven daughters. Their youngest child, Irene, died at the age of five because of burns received in the fire that consumed their home in 1926.

The Toews family moved to Eigenheim, Saskatchewan, in 1904. There David began his nearly two decades as teacher and principal at the German-English Academy at Rosthern, which he founded. In 1901 he had been elected to the ministry of the Rosenort Mennonite Church at Rosthern, and in 1913 he became an elder (bishop). In his teaching he was considered highly successful; his students loved and respected him. When pastoral duties during World War I demanded more of his time, he resigned as principal of the school. He continued as a board member until a few years before his death in 1947.

Toews served the Canadian General Conference Mennonite Church as secretary and chairman. At business sessions, he was able to grasp the essentials of a subject and present them in digested form so that appropriate resolutions could be drawn up. His work often took him to Ottawa, Regina, Winnipeg, and Chicago. He attended the Mennonite World Conferences of 1930 and 1936. Toews was well qualified for these travels—self-confident, frank, trustworthy, and resolute in his dealings. Margarete made his church work possible by supervising the affairs of the household, even though she suffered from trachoma, nearly loosing her eyesight.

David Toews was elected treasurer of funds for several projects. In this capacity he was usually responsible for gathering money. In these tasks, he was patient, cheerful, and optimistic, always trusting that the money would be forthcoming. That, however, was not always the case, and not everyone shared his optimism.

In 1918 and 1919, reports began to circulate about the terror of the Russian Revolution and the suffering of Mennonites there. By the hundreds, Mennonites gathered in Canada and the United States to hear about the plight of their sisters and brothers in Russia. Committees were organized to offer assistance. Money was collected and sent to Russia. Orie Miller, Clayton Kratz, Arthur Slagel, and Alvin J. Miller became the church's agents to administer the relief funds and materials.

Delegations from Russia came to speak firsthand about the suffering. They also presented their people's need to immigrate to North America. American immigration officials soon made it clear that the United States would not accept them, despite the claim inscribed on the Statue of Liberty in New York's harbor: "Give me your tired, your poor, . . . yearning to breathe free." Would Canada's doors be open?

God's call came to David Toews. Though it would have been far easier to continue his work in the congregation and the school at Rosthern, his deep empathy for his brothers and sisters in distress would not let him ignore them. Most people thought the solution was to send relief overseas; Toews was soon convinced that the best solution was to bring the people to Canada. It grieved him that his convictions were not shared in the States, where it was said that the refugees should be sent to Mexico. Canadians also had their doubts, and so did the Canadian government.

After World War I, an Order in Council was issued, rejecting any more immigration to Canada. How could that order be overruled? The political campaign of 1922-23 was in progress, and the Liberal party under the leadership of Mackenzie King promised that, if he were elected, his government would rescind the objectionable Order in Council. Would it happen? The Liberals *were* elected, and the discriminatory laws *were* repealed. The doors were opened to Mennonite refugees. The Canadian Pacific Railway

Company agreed to provide transportation for the immigrants on credit granted under favorable terms.

There were additional problems: How would the immigrants be received, cared for, and settled? H. H. Ewert proposed that a mortgage be floated to purchase the land of the Old Colony Mennonites in Manitoba. It would take a long time. Furthermore, who would provide the money? A. A. Friesen and a lawyer, A. C. March of Saskatoon, suggested another plan: create a stock company with total shares of ten million dollars to finance the entire project. This workable plan was approved, and a charter was secured for a stock company.

Meanwhile, Toews gave up his position at the Heidelberg public school to become chairman of the Canadian Board of Colonization. It was a full-time job. The board named A. A. Friesen as its secretary and established its headquarters in Rosthern. Toews managed the finances for the 1923-30 migration of Russian Mennonites to Canada. This was by far the greatest test of his patience, optimism, and faith. Though he said he was *not* a businessman, he handled millions of dollars, giving his personal guarantee to the Canadian government that the *Reiseschuld* (travel debt) would be repaid.

The first contact with the railroad provided for the transportation of three thousand people in 1923. When this contract was first issued in Montreal in July 1922, a great disappointment came with it. The transportation rates were excessively high, and the entire debt was to be repaid in six months!

Toews would not give up. He went back to Ottawa. When asked who would guarantee that the loan would be repaid, he responded, "*I* guarantee it!" Nobody laughed, though they all knew that he was as poor as a church mouse. By that time, they also knew he could be trusted. David Toews signed his name to the fateful document and became the personal guarantor for ten million dollars.

As arrangements progressed, the churches became

uneasy. Who were these immigrants? Could they be trusted? Who would speak for them? Who would guarantee that the loans would be repaid? Even in the States where Toews hoped for so much help, his motives were misinterpreted. In Canada, some congregations in Saskatchewan refused to help. Friends became enemies.

Repeatedly Toews had to explain that the Board of Colonization was responsible; no one individual or church would be held accountable; the contract was a "gentlemen's agreement." This explanation satisfied many but not all. One is reminded of Moses, plagued by the murmuring of his own people.

With the permission of Canada, the immigrants now could come. However, the Old Colonist land had not been bought, and the ten-million-dollar corporation did not materialize. Toews said, "Mennonites give freely, but if they suspect a business enterprise is involved, they are distrustful." His efforts to raise money for the ten-million-dollar project also met with failure in the United States. The people refused because they thought the immigrants should go to Mexico.

Then another issue arose: If our plans are not realized, the contract with the Canadian Pacific Railway will be annulled! "No," declared Toews emphatically, "the contract will not be annulled!" In spite of persistent criticism, Toews was always courteous in his responses. Finally, when it became clear that Mexico was not an option, U.S. Mennonites supported the migration to Canada.

The coming of the first immigrants was delayed, but finally they came. They landed in Quebec on July 17, 1923, and arrived in Rosthern by July 21. The coming of the first six hundred immigrants caused a great commotion and a hosting challenge. But by evening, all had been fed and cared for.

Other immigrants soon followed: 2,759 in 1923, and 5,048 in 1924. Even more followed, so that by 1930, a grand total of 20,201 Russian Mennonite refugees had come to the promised land of Canada.

Those who brought some money along were able to pay for their passage. After the first immigrants were settled, they, in turn, helped newer immigrants.

In September 1925, David and Margarete celebrated the silver anniversary of their wedding. It seemed but a minor interlude in his mission to resettle the refugees. From February to April of 1926, Toews traveled to Europe to visit refugees detained in Germany. Back in Canada, the new arrivals had to be settled. Regulations did not permit them to take up urban occupations, so they had to live in the country, many under unfavorable conditions.

By 1927 Soviet Russia imposed more difficulties on emigration and, eventually, the migration was halted. Canada, because of the Depression and unemployment, refused to accept more immigrants. So the movement came to a close in 1930. At first, Toews could not accept the sudden termination, but he was forced to acknowledge that the stream of refugees from "the land of terror" to Canada had ended. The "Iron Curtain" had slammed shut.

There was already enough work. Over twenty thousand new settlers were scattered over the land from Ontario to Alberta. Supplying clothes, organizing churches, ordaining elders and ministers, visiting the sick—what a task it was! And the travel debt still needed to be paid! It was taking so long to repay it. Would he ever see the final dollar? It was not likely.

Eventually, it became the lot of C. F. Klassen to collect the remaining travel debt of over two million dollars. Hindered by the Great Depression of the 1930s, it took Klassen twenty-five years to collect the entire debt. At last the day came when Pastor J. J. Thiessen took the good news to the old and tired David Toews.

"The entire travel debt and all the interest has been repaid," Thiessen told Toews.

At first Toews would not believe it. He chided Thiessen: "I know you all feel sorry for me, since I gave my word that the debt would be paid. You know I can't die until it is paid."

Thiessen cupped his hands to the ears of the hard-of-hearing brother and repeated the good news once more. David Toews sat back in his rocker. With tears soaking his beard, he kept saying again and again, "Gott sei Dank! Thank you, God."[19]

The covered wagon of the great Western migration.
INSET Homesteaders holding their claim.

The Cherokee Run

Diedrich L. Dalke

Pioneering has fascinated European Americans since they first set foot on American soil. New and cheaper farmland lured farmers and adventurers westward each time new territories were opened for settlement. In northcentral Oklahoma, the Cherokee Outlet was one of the last frontiers in the continental United States. Among the one hundred thousand land "boomers" rushing to stake new claims in 1893 were a few European American Mennonites. They seemed to care little that Native Americans were being displaced once again, even though General Conference Mennonite "foreign" missionaries were then living among the Cheyenne and the Apache. This story is told from the vantage point of a homesteader's son, who also recounts the difficult early years of farming.

A T A QUARTER to twelve, thousands of eager land seekers were all set for the race that has been called the greatest race in history. It was a race for homesteads in the Cherokee Outlet of Oklahoma, more commonly known as the "Cherokee Strip." In May 1893, after years of pressure by "boomers," the United States purchased the Outlet for eight million dollars from the Cherokee Indians. This was likely a losing deal for the Indians, who had become conditioned to

63

disappointments in earlier negotiations with the U.S. government.

In August, President Grover Cleveland proclaimed the Outlet ready for settlement. The date for the opening was set for September 16, 1893.

The Outlet was a tract of land in Northwestern Oklahoma Territory extending fifty-eight miles south from the Kansas line and running 226 miles west along that line from the ninety-sixth to the one hundredth meridian.

For five days or more, people from many places assembled at the border to register and make preparations for the takeoff. Around sixty-five thousand persons, some of them women, were ready to make the run from northern centers in Kansas such as Arkansas City, Caldwell, Kiowa, and Hunnewell; thirty-seven thousand were waiting at southern centers of Hennesey, Arlando, and Stillwater in Oklahoma.

At last it was twelve o'clock! The guards promptly fired the signal guns. With many whoops and hollers, the masses of humanity surged forward, rushing pell-mell into the Outlet! They stampeded ahead on horseback and in or on every kind of horse-drawn vehicle—buggies, spring wagons, surreys, buckboards, carts, wagons with and without covers, wagon running gears (without bed or box) or parts of them, trains, and a few on bicycles.

How many Mennonites took part in the race probably cannot be determined. The settlements at Menno, Medford, Fairview, Orienta, Lahoma, Kremlin, and others may have had their beginnings in this race.

My father, Abraham Dalke, a blacksmith from Henderson, Nebraska, made the run from Caldwell on a train that he described as being made up of forty-two cattle cars with passengers packed inside, somewhat like posts on end. Passengers completely covered the tops of the cars, with some clinging to the sides wherever they could find a hand-hold and toehold! The train was powered by three locomotives. At first it lagged behind those on horseback and in assorted vehicles; later it overtook them and traveled ahead too fast for safe jumping off. However, some took the risk safely; others suffered skin abrasions, bruises, and even broken bones.

This was not an ordinary horse race. There were actually two races, one from the north and one from the south. The races offered prizes for thousands who staked a claim somewhere along the course. There were losers too, those who failed to stake a claim; those who found they had made their stake on school land (four sections to a township); and those who lost out to rival claimants.

In two hours, riders and trains from opposite directions met near the middle, and the race was over. In two hours, nearly fifty thousand homesteads had claimants on them, and the towns along the railroads were populated! There remained only primitive first nights in the open and the detail of filing at a land office to legalize the claim. The land agents issued numbers so people wouldn't have to stand in line indefinitely; yet there were days of waiting.

Since Father did not jump off the train, he was one of the losers, but he did not lose his interest in the Outlet. He and Isaac Regier, a hardware dealer in Henderson, made a train trip to Enid in early spring. My dad returned with a lease on a school quarter section, and Regier paid a man to relinquish the claim he had filed on a homestead.

Mennonites who came early to the Enid vicinity later leased school land, rented a farm, or purchased relinquishments. Many who made the race were willing to sell for eight hundred to a thousand dollars. They had experienced enough of drought, poor crops, and hard times.

Having loaded our *Siebensachen* (belongings) and some of Isaac Regier's, Father and I boarded the immigrant car. After two cold nights, we reached Enid, later called North Enid, on May 16, 1894. We were the second Mennonite family to arrive. Bernhard M. Regier had arrived a few months earlier. He and two sons were there to met us and helped drive the cows we brought to the Isaac Regier farm, where the family lived in a one-room dugout, rather primitive and crowded living for a family with nine children.

The third family to arrive that year was Gerhard K. Fast with George and Katie, and the fourth was the Peter Janzen family, all from Henderson. The Janzen family came overland, with their goods loaded on a hayrack that the family followed closely in a buggy. How anxiously we looked for their arrival! How expectantly we walked to North Enid for a letter, sometimes not finding any! Finally the hayrack drawn by two ill-matched mules came in sight as it topped the hill on the Chisholm Trail. At last they were here, after nearly three weeks of traveling.

There was a lot of movement to and from the Outlet for a period of five or more years. In 1895 Isaac Regier arrived by rail. One day Peter P. Regier with his bride, Mary Schellenberg of Buhler, Kansas, drove by our place in a covered wagon, going to their new home nearby.

Those who made the run and those who moved to the Outlet one, two, or three years after the opening had to start farming from scratch. There were dugout shelters to be made; houses, sheds, and barns to build, good ones or makeshift, as finances might dictate; wells and cellars or caves to dig for protection against tornadoes and for storing vegetables and keeping dairy products in a cool place. Then too, the prairie had to be broken if there was to be any crop.

We used a grasshopper plow to break the prairie. It had a short low beam and four adjustable rods that functioned like a moldboard. When properly adjusted it cut, lifted, turned over, and laid the sod back upside down, smoothly and without a break, into the furrow of the previous round.

It was fun to walk behind the grasshopper, usually pulled by two horses. The cutting of the thick mat of grass roots made a pleasant sound. The sod turned over gracefully and fell into place so easily. But watch out for that shoestring weed! Its roots might cause the plow to jump out, and then there would be the job of pulling it backward, with the attached doubletree adding its weight, and sometimes the horses would also have to be pulled back to start over again.

Sod broken in the spring could be planted with kaffir corn, milo, maize, cane, watermelons, sweet potatoes and turnips, or castor beans. For fall planting of wheat, the sod was double disked before sowing with a drill.

The dry years that prevailed after the land run did not bring the results anticipated from a farm in the Outlet. Father pastured his cows on fifty-three acres of wheat in the winter of 1894-95. Dry weather caught the crop when it was ready to head out, with dire results. What a stunted harvest—short straw and small shriveled heads, some not fully out of the boot! It was not worth cutting, but Father needed seed, or thought he did, for another try. It had to be cut somehow.

Father attached a sheet metal platform to the sickle bar of the mowing machine. While my oldest brother drove the horses, my father walked beside the mower and raked the cut grain farther back on the platform. When it was full, he pushed the load off, forming windrows.

By agreeing to pay a setting fee, he succeeded in getting a thresher man to thresh the two small stacks. He got only one bushel per acre! This was our reward for all the work, days and days of it, not to mention the fact that he had sown a bushel and a peck per acre. However, he was glad to get the seed and to trade blacksmithing services for enough more wheat to sow seventy-five acres.

The harvest of the second crop was better but still not good. When two headers cut the grain in a day and a half, they were through harvesting and all the wheat was in stacks. A horse-powered machine was engaged to thresh the wheat. It was interesting to watch the men set this machine. The horsepower had to be braced and staked down so it could sustain the reaction and stay in proper position. Two men accomplished this by alternately driving iron-ringed wooden stakes with sledges, forcing them into the ground in less than a minute.

The sweeps were unloaded and inserted into the square holders provided for them on the main power wheel. Brace rods were fastened to them. Tumbling rods were coupled with knuckles, and tumbling rod boxes were anchored to the ground with stakes. The power was now ready for the five teams that the team owners drove to their places, one team to a sweep, each owner holding a doubletree with all tugs attached in one hand and handling the reins with the other.

When the teams were hitched, the driver took his place on the platform and started the horses. Slowly the power began to turn the tumbling rods, the momentum gradually increased, and the horses kept going round and round while the hum of the machinery increased in pitch and changed, now higher, now lower, as the feeder varied his feeding or failed to control it properly. We threshed only four bushels per acre. We hoped the next harvest would be better.[20]

We and the other eager land boomers, who raced into the Cherokee Outlet to claim a homestead on September 16, 1893, hoped for more than four bushels of wheat per acre. We dreamed of prosperity and abundance. But home-steading, creating a new farm on the prairies, was always a risk. It was a risk one hundred thousand optimistic people were willing to take.

Annie Funk Memorial School: to multiply her efforts many times over.

INSET Annie C. Funk: confident that "our heavenly Father is as near to us on sea as on land."

Annie Funk, the *Titanic*, and a School in India

Christena Duerksen

*By the turn of the century, both the Mennonite Church
and the General Conference Mennonite Church had
established overseas missions in India. Twenty years earlier the General Conference Mennonite Church had sent
its first "foreign" missionaries to Indian Territory, in
what is now Oklahoma. As a young girl, Annie Funk
knew she wanted to be a missionary. The stories missionaries told when they visited the Hereford General
Conference Mennonite Church in Bally, Pennsylvania,
fascinated her. Her fascination was nurtured into a call
to serve in India in 1908. Her work and her life were cut
short by a tragedy that shocked the world—the sinking
of the* Titanic *in the icy waters of the North
Atlantic Ocean.*

DOWN BY THE island's edge, an Indian stepped out of a
small ferryboat. He hurried up the steep bank and came
straight to a group of missionaries seated in front of a tent.
In his hands he carried an envelope that he handed to Annie
C. Funk. It was a cable message from the homeland. The
sight of a cable always made the heart beat faster. It can so
easily carry disturbing news. This one did.

The message came from Annie Funk's pastor in

71

Pennsylvania, telling her to come home at once. It even named the two ships on which they had purchased passage for her. The reason: Annie's mother was very ill.

The three missionaries looked at each other in amazement. As their thoughts cleared, they realized that there were only three days in which to pack and get to Bombay, and they were not even at home. They had come to Madjughat Island to prepare for a convention. The first train they could take to get back to Janjgir left in the evening, from a small station seven or more miles from the island. P. W. Penner could not leave his work, but Mathilde Penner would go with Annie to help her.

Hastily, they packed their belongings. Just before sunset, the two women were jogging along the dusty road in a springless oxcart. Anxiety clutched at Annie's heart. Letters had told of mother's ill health for some time. Would she get home in time?

Early the next morning, all was hustle and bustle as the two women had boxes and trunks brought out of storerooms and started sorting, choosing, and packing. Annie expected to be back after a brief furlough. But it hurt to leave in such a hurry. No time for a farewell service. As the news spread, many of her Indian friends came to express their sympathy and love.

In India it was already getting hot, yet they knew that on the Atlantic, it would still be cold. Since Annie had no suitable coat, Mathilde urged her to take her own good black coat. When all was packed, Annie boarded the train. As Mathilde saw Annie standing in the coach door, waving good-bye, she was cheered by Annie's promise, "I'll be back soon." The whistle blew, the train started, swung around the curve, and disappeared from view. Annie was gone—never to return.

In the train, Annie settled down for the tedious, long, dusty journey to Bombay—two nights and a day of travel. Her black hair, neatly combed, and her dark eyes made her all the more acceptable to the people she had come to serve. As the train rumbled along, she had time to review the almost six years she had spent in India. Humorous incidents, heartbreaking experiences, times of testing, and times of great blessing came to mind.

The climate had never bothered her much. She had not minded the heat as others did, though she wrote to friends that the hot weather made her lazy. In winter months she had found woolen bed socks to be comfortable. During the rains, even dusty Janjgir had been clothed with beautiful green grass and flowering shrubs.

There was so much that was beautiful in this land of India: flowering trees and shrubs, luscious fruits of many kinds, glorious sunrises and sunsets, and waving fields of growing rice that turned to gold as the harvest set in.

How much easier it had become when she could finally talk to people in their language. The hours with the old language teacher had been interesting. Sometimes he had told her she was doing well. At other times he had shaken his head and said, "I wish you had studied better." Fellow missionaries had told her that she would get along faster if she were not so hesitant to use what she already knew. It was easier talking to the children. But she knew it would be a lifelong job to master a language such as Hindi.

On March 19, 1912, she was one of the passengers sailing for England on the *SS Persian*. Sitting in her steamer chair, she found her thoughts going back to the girls' school that had been her special charge. She could smile now as she thought of the first day of school. She had wanted to start without any fuss, but the leaders of the village had insisted on proper opening ceremonies.

The time had been set for eight o'clock in the morning. Only the *malguzar* (village owner) and one government official had arrived on time. Annie and Susanna Kroeker had grown tired of waiting. Finally, at ten o'clock, the rest of the "important" people had come. One of the speakers had said,

"All great women can read," and had cited Queen Victoria as a shining example. Judging by the comparatively small number of girls who had come to school, Annie was afraid that Janjgir would have few great women.

The little girls who had come to school had done fairly well. But there were none over twelve years of age. So many things were allowed to interfere. Sometimes the girls were unruly. Sometimes they were absent—one sick, another caring for the baby, and another running away to hide. Sometimes one was asked for marriage and needed to stay indoors from then on. Still another would stay home because a close relative had died. When that happened, all in the household were considered unclean, and no books could be handled.

There had, however, been a happier side. The girls had seemed to like the Bible stories and songs. They had learned many Bible verses. Annie's prayer had been that they might come to know the Savior. Because they came from Hindu homes, Annie wondered what chance the girls had to follow the Christian teachings they received in school.

She thought of Maina Bai, the Marathi Brahmin woman, who was her monitor. Every morning she made the rounds of the girls' homes to take the girls to school. When school was dismissed, she marched them back home. How trying she had been at times! Annie would have rejoiced if she could have seen many years later that Maina Bai was counted among the Christians.

As the ship continued westward, her thoughts went back less frequently to the land she had left and began to reach out to the land to which she was returning. Often she would picture the farm home of her childhood in the Butter Valley, with her mother busy about the house, the girls doing their appointed tasks, and her father and brother busy in the fields or the barn. She remembered the Sunday morning rides to Hereford General Conference Mennonite Church near Bally, along three miles of shaded roads. How good it would feel to sit on the familiar church benches again.

It would be so satisfying to talk about India to those who were interested: her pastor, mission board members, and friends with whom she had been in school at Northfield. Sometimes, when letters were slow in coming, she had been tempted to think they had all forgotten her.

Because of the urgency for her to reach home, her route had been planned to allow her to travel by train across Europe from Brindisi, Italy, while the *SS Persian* made its more leisurely way around Gibraltar and up the coast.

When she reached England, she was disturbed to find that the *SS Haverford* would be delayed for six or more days because of a coal strike. Should she wait that long? Might there be another ship she could take?

Thomas Cook and Sons, who made travel arrangements for her, suggested that by paying extra fare she could get second-class passage on the *SS Titanic*, the new palace of the seas. Before the *Haverford* would sail, she would already be home. Should she take that opportunity?

As the *Titanic* steamed out of Southampton harbor, Annie wrote a hurried letter to her fellow missionaries in India, which she sent back to land by pilot boat. In it she said, "I had to get out a few more gold pieces (to pay for passage on this boat), but I gladly did that to get home six days earlier, and will let my people know from New York."

She went on to express her surprise at the beauty and luxury of the great ocean palace and her pleasure at being so near home. She expressed no uneasiness regarding the journey. When she had sailed to India, she had told friends, "Our heavenly Father is as near to us on sea as on land. My trust is in him, and I have no fear." She had the same confidence now.

Christians on board a ship soon find each other, and it must have been so for Annie. Then came that fateful night! The "unsinkable," mighty *Titanic* sank into the icy waters of the North Atlantic Ocean.

At home, friends and relatives were counting the days until the *Haverford* would arrive. Letters of welcome had been sent to meet her in England, but little did they know that these had not reached her.

On April 15, the whole world was shocked by the news of the sinking of the "invincible" *Titanic*. The community at Bally, Pennsylvania, was stunned when Annie Funk's name appeared among the names of those who were missing. Why had she been on this ship? Could it be another Annie C. Funk? Letters of inquiry to the ship's company brought little information.

Hoping against hope, friends and relatives waited. But there was no mistake. Annie Funk did not come home. What had happened in those last hours?

In one story of the tragedy, there is a short paragraph that reads, "Outside on the decks, the crowd still waited; the band still played. A few prayed with Thomas R. Byles, a minister and second-class passenger. Others seemed lost in thought." Surely Annie was among the "few" who prayed.

Her pastor, A. S. Shelly wrote, "We counted on the good results to flow from her personal testimony among us during the months of her furlough, . . . but we stand bereft of all our expectations."

Memorial services were held in many Mennonite churches. Her mother, because of whose illness Annie was hurrying home, was sufficiently recovered to attend Annie's memorial service at Hereford. The next spring, the Eastern District Conference unveiled a memorial marker in the cemetery of her home congregation.

When money was still being sent for her memorial, it was forwarded to India. There another memorial was built. It was not a stone set in a cemetery. It was a two-story brick school building, capable of holding more girls than Annie had ever seen in her little school. A plaque on the outer wall was inscribed with the new name: *Annie Funk Memorial School.* During its years of operation, many girls were trained to become teachers, nurses, and Christian disciples. Annie Funk's efforts were multiplied many times over.[21]

Johann J. and Elisabeth (Stucky) Schrag with their ten children in more peaceful times, about 1912.

INSET At the crossroads: a World War I anti-German political cartoon from the *New York Evening Telegram*.

Showdown in Burrton, Kansas

James C. Juhnke

When World War I broke out, Mennonites discovered they were considered enemies by their neighbors and business associates. Their German origins, even if generations removed, their German language and culture, and their pacifism made them suspect. In some communities, patriotic citizen groups harassed "slackers" by throwing yellow paint on houses and meetinghouses, committing arson, tarring and feathering pacifists, and threatening death by hanging. In this story Swiss Volhynian Mennonite John Schrag finds himself in the hands of such a patriotic mob.

THE JOHN SCHRAG espionage case was the dramatic climax to the dilemma of Kansas Mennonites in World War I. John Schrag was chosen to be the symbol and the bearer of the American community's mistrust and hatred of German-speaking pacifists in the tense days of 1918.

John Schrag was a believer in those simple and durable virtues that made Mennonites highly prized citizens on the Kansas frontier. He was thirteen years old when his family emigrated from Volhynia, Russia, to central Kansas in 1874. In his teens, he helped his father build a grain mill on the banks of the Little Arkansas River in Harvey County.[22] From his father, he learned the value of hard work, the love of the soil, and the wisdom of careful investment.

From the Mennonite faith and tradition, Schrag knew that God generously rewards his faithful laboring servants. Schrag's rise as a prosperous farmer with a large family and extensive landholdings was as natural as the economic and social success of the Mennonite community in the first decades after arrival in the new country.

The Mennonite role as outstanding and valuable citizens received an unforgettable jolt when the United States entered World War I in 1917. It suddenly became a requirement of acceptable American citizenship to support the war and to hate Germany. The Mennonites failed on both counts. They could not support the war because their religious faith taught them nonresistance, a doctrine whose practical expression included a claim for exemption from military service. They could not hate Germany because Mennonites themselves were of German background and loved the German language and culture as preserved in their homes, schools, and churches.

Their sympathies in the European war had been demonstrated in their collections of money for the German Red Cross.[23] Mennonites could not be acceptable citizens in America during World War I unless they gave up their German culture and their doctrine of nonresistance.

The war bond drives became the test of loyal citizenship in the local community. Faced alternatively with persuasion and intimidation by local Loyalty Leagues, many Mennonites reconciled their nonresistance with the purchase of the bonds. After all, reasoned Henry Peter Krehbiel, member of the Western District Committee on Exemptions, a war bond is a kind of tax, and Jesus told us to pay our taxes.[24] But John Schrag was not convinced. Buying bonds was supporting the war, and he would not support the war. That was that.

On November 11, 1918, a group of patriotic citizens in

Burrton, Kansas, decided that the time was ripe for a showdown. "We was out to convert these slackers into patriots,"
said one of them later.[25] Five carloads of men drove eleven
miles to the Schrag farm near the Alta Mill to get Schrag to
join the Armistice Day festivities in Burrton. Schrag's boys,
sensing trouble, refused to say where their father was, but
the Burrton men found him after ransacking the farmstead
and forcing their way into the house. Schrag offered neither
argument nor resistance. He went along in the hope that a
measure of cooperation would help avoid physical violence.[26]

In Burrton, a crowd quickly gathered as the citizens con-
fronted Schrag with their real reason for bringing him to
town. He must buy war bonds now or face the consequences.
Schrag offered to contribute two hundred dollars to the Red
Cross and the Salvation Army,[27] but this was not sufficient.

They demanded that he salute the American flag and
carry the flag through town at the head of a parade. But
Schrag quietly and firmly refused to cooperate. The flag
thrust into his hand fell to the ground. Someone shouted,
"He stepped on the flag!" The crowd suddenly became an
enraged mob.

They sprinkled and poured yellow paint on their victim,
rubbing it into his scalp and beard until he resembled "a big
cheese or yellow squash or pumpkin after the autumnal
ripening."[28] They led him to the city jail. Someone ran for a
rope to hang him, but Tom Roberts, the head of the local
Anti-Horse-Thief Association, courageously stood before the
jail door, brandishing a gun, and saying, "If you take this
man out of jail, you take him over my dead body."
Temporarily frustrated, the indignant citizens made plans to
return that night, force the jail open, and hang this so-called
traitor.

Meanwhile, Schrag was placed in a chair on a raised platform in the jail, so passersby could view the humiliated man
through the window in the jail door. One repentant member

of the mob later testified to Schrag's calmness throughout the ordeal: "If ever a man looked like Christ, he did."[29]

Schrag was finally rescued from the Burrton crusaders for American democracy by the Harvey County sheriff, who came that evening to take him to the county jail in Newton for cleaning and safekeeping. Before he was released, Schrag was informed that he was to be tried in court for violation of the Espionage Act. It was against the law to desecrate the flag of the United States.

Local newspaper accounts of the incident failed to defend the rights of the victim. The weekly Burrton *Graphic* on November 14 saw in the event "a pungent and durable reminder that loyalty is a necessary prerequisite to life in this community. We must be all Americans."[30] The Hutchinson *News* article said that "a petition is being circulated to have him [Schrag] deported to Germany, his native land. This country is fast becoming an unhealthy place for 'slackers' of any kind."[31]

The Newton *Evening Kansan-Republican* suggested that if a federal court would find Schrag guilty, "it would undoubtedly mean the confiscation of his property and his deportation."[32] On the week of his hearing in Wichita, the editor of the Burrton *Graphic* published a list: "Some Things Residents of Burrton Should Be Thankful For." In the list was "That we as a people are more tolerant of others' foibles."[33]

The case against Schrag was heard in the Wichita federal courtrooms by U.S. Commissioner C. Shearman on December 9. Five Burrton citizens presented fifty typewritten pages of evidence to prove Schrag's disloyalty and desecration of the flag. For his defense, Schrag retained the services of a Jewish lawyer named Schulz. Commissioner Shearman took the case under advisement and promised that the decision would be made shortly.

The decision, handed down on December 24, was that Schrag was not guilty and should not be bound over for federal trial. But Commissioner Shearman did say that "Schrag could not have gone closer to a violation of the espionage act if he had had a hundred lawyers at his side to advise him."[34]

Schrag in fact had not willfully desecrated the flag. Nothing in the Espionage Act required one to salute the flag. Schrag's words that supposedly slandered the flag had been spoken in German, so none of the monolingual plaintiffs could prove any guilt.

The Newton *Evening Kansan-Republican*, frustrated by the acquittal of this "bull-headed" man, suggested that the case "should certainly make plain to any thinking person the viciousness that exists in the encouragement of the German language as a means of communication in America. . . . The melting pot cannot exercise its proper functions when such things are allowed."[35]

The Mennonite newspapers in central Kansas, intimidated into silence, did not come to Schrag's defense and did not even mention the incident or the hearing as an item of news. After the commissioner's decision, however, C. E. Krehbiel, editor of *Der Herold* (Newton), wrote an editorial, "Mob Power," that clearly referred to the Schrag case, although it mentioned no specific names or events. In cases of mob violence, wrote Krehbiel, either the mob or the abused person is guilty. If the court of justice decides that the victim is innocent, the only conclusion is that the mob is guilty. Readers were to make their own applications.[36]

Schrag's attorney encouraged him to bring charges against his persecutors, but Schrag declined. Such an action would have violated the Mennonite principles of nonresistance. Nevertheless, in the months after the Schrag affair, the nonresistant German-Mennonites had no scruples against clamping an economic boycott on the town of Burrton.[37] The boycott was not organized systematically, but it was effective in disrupting the trade of Burrton businessmen who were dependent upon the commerce of German-Mennonite farmers. The legacy of tension and hatred generated by the event would be remembered for decades to come.

The experience of the Mennonites in World War I hardly had a salutary effect on the processes of the American melting pot. In the years after the war, the Mennonites were driven to a defensive retrenchment, to a renewed awareness of their distinctiveness as Mennonites. Though they gradually abandoned their German language and some German cultural traits, the war experiences forced them to a reconsideration and reaffirmation of the doctrine of nonresistance. As long as Mennonites held to that doctrine, they would be a thorn in the flesh of American nationalists.

The witness of John Schrag, and of other Mennonites who refused to compromise their doctrine of nonresistance during wartime, can serve as a reminder of the Anabaptist heritage of steadfastness in the face of persecution.[38]

Arming for defense: the Selbstschutz for the villages Blumenort, Tiege, and Ohrloff of the Molotschna Colony, Russia.

INSET Nestor Makhno.

Revolution in Russia

Gerhard Lohrenz

Few experiences in the twentieth century have been as traumatic for European Mennonites as the chaos of the Bolshevik Revolution in Russia in 1917. Invited to Russia in 1789 by Czarina Catherine the Great, Mennonites lived in colonies and on large estates. Their isolation from Russian society and their uncommon wealth made Mennonites targets of the revolutionaries. Especially notorious among the plundering, raping bands of outlaws in southern Ukraine, was the Makhnovtsy, led by Nestor Makhno. Regarded today as a Ukranian national hero, the name Makhno struck fear into many Mennonite families. Mennonites were tempted to aban- don their nonresistance and to meet violence with violence, as this story reveals.

T HE TURBULENT MONTHS following the Russian Revolution of March 1917 opened the jails of Russia and brought untold thousands out of the penitentiaries of Siberia. All these men claimed to have suffered innocently. They were thirsting for revenge and longing to continue their lives of crime that had been interrupted by their imprison- ment.

In addition to the release of these prisoners, another hardened array of men found themselves "freed" and also forced their violence upon the country. This group was composed of citizens who for years had been fighting on the wartime front. Bloodshed and cruelty had become everyday affairs to them. Now they began to murder their officers and plunder the storehouses of the government. In heavily armed bands under their own chosen leaders, they returned to the interior of the country.

In this interior where chaos ruled, there was yet a third group, the Russian peasants. They were hearing the wild schemes of agitators of various extreme political parties. After generations of illiteracy and oppression, they were suddenly free, armed, and in the absolute majority. The peasants nursed a historic grudge against those who had oppressed them. In many cases, their ignorance and lack of experience in self-determination made them prey to these skilled and unscrupulous agitators.

The Russian masses did not go wild, but thousands of individuals did. The resulting uprisings were distinguished by their destructiveness, cruelty, and the blind murder of all whose station of life was above that of the common peasants.

As these chaotic elements were unleashed, Russia was in flames, particularly the rich south. Many bands, often numbering into the thousands, roamed the country, claiming to be fighters for freedom and justice. In reality, they were nothing more than the dregs of society, aiming at nothing better than plunder, murder, and rape. One of the largest and most dreadful of these bands was led by Nestor Makhno. Soon he came to be known as Batyko Makhno (BAH-tee-kuh mach-NAW; Ukrainian for "Daddy Makhno"), and his followers were called *Makhnovtsy* (mach-NOV-tsee).

Makhno was born in 1889 in southern Russia. His parents were poor, and Nestor had to serve the wealthy from childhood on. He learned to hate them. At the age of seventeen, he took part in the upheaval of 1905. In 1908 he was caught and condemned to the penitentiary for life. Only his youth saved him from the hanging rope.

In the penitentiary he became even more hardened as his bitterness grew. When the 1917 Revolution came, it set him free, and he returned to his home district in southern Russia. Intelligent, cunning, cruel, sensuous, and burning with hatred for all those above his peasant status, he became the acknowledged and highly admired leader of a band of desperadoes who would stop at nothing. Any meanness and cruelty perpetrated upon the wealthy, the educated, or anyone who in any way could be associated with the czarist government or the former upper class—it all seemed to Makhno and his followers as fair sport.

Makhno and his followers claimed to be anarchists, opposed to any and every form of government. The peasants and laborers were to rule themselves through their own elected committees. No central government was necessary because all were brothers. Police forces, government officials, and prisons were evil institutions that had to be destroyed.

In September 1919 near the city of Umany, the forces of Makhno won a great victory over the White (anti-Communist) Army. As a consequence, immense territories of southern Russia fell into the hand of these adventurers. Makhno immediately sent out his forces in various directions, with orders to cleanse the country of all the people who might be a hindrance to the development of an anarchist paradise. Historian Peter Arshinov, a leading anarchist terrorist and a colleague of Makhno, wrote of this event:

Not hesitating for a minute, Makhno sent his armies into three directions. As a broom of destiny, he went through the villages, the towns, and cities, and swept out every spirit of exploitation and slavery. Landed proprietors, wealthy peasants, policemen, ministers, elders, hidden officers—they all fell as victims along the path the Makhnovtsy were traveling. Prisons, police, and commissar offices—the symbols of national slavery—

were destroyed. Anyone exposed as an offender against the peasants or laborers perished. The groups that felt the severity of this act most were the landed proprietors and the well-to-do peasants *(kulaks)*.[39]

Though Makhno's bands and other lawless groups first attacked the educated and the upper class, German villages would be next. Southern Russia had hundreds of German villages: Mennonite, Lutheran, Catholic, and others. These Germans were of a more developed culture, more energetic and practical than the Russian peasants. They were generally well-to-do and had spacious homes surrounded by lovely gardens. Beautiful horses in great number were found in the stables of these villages. Homes were well stocked with all of the necessities of life.

These Germans had not intermarried with their Russian neighbors and were seen as superior to the peasants. The German settlers employed many Russian laborers, but the peasants often felt exploited. In addition, since 1914 the Russian press had carried on a negative campaign against all German-speaking citizens. World War I had created a hatred of all Germans.

All these reasons combined made the German villages of Russia a mecca for armed bandits. Here they could perpetrate their abominable deeds, find rich plunder, and still pretend to have some laudable excuse for all their destructive deeds. Since the Mennonites as a group belonged to the successful German farmers, their extermination was a foregone conclusion. In the eyes of the Makhno bands, the simple fact that they were prosperous justified their death sentences.

In desperation, some of the villages, including some of the Mennonite villages, resorted to armed resistance. Some fellow Mennonites were critical of this response and later suggested that subsequent massacres in some of these villages would never have occurred had Mennonites not attempted such resistance. Perhaps so and perhaps not.

It is impossible to describe all the crimes committed in the German villages of southern Russia. As an illustration, consider the Mennonite settlement of Zagradovka. This area consisted of fifteen villages with a total Mennonite population of 4,067.

From November 29 to December 1, 1919, one of Makhno's bands overran six villages of this settlement. The Makhnovtsy murdered two hundred individuals. Many others were wounded and crippled for life. Three widowers, seventy-two widows, and many orphans were left behind. The band burned to the ground the whole village of Münsterberg and seventy-five homesteads in the other villages. Hundreds of horses and cows perished in the burning buildings. The Makhnovtsy shamefully violated many women, old and young. They hauled away great quantities of goods of all descriptions.

Had these people in some way provoked this fate? This hardly seems to be the case. Though Münsterberg was not poor, it was one of the poorer villages of the settlement. In addition, I know that many of the inhabitants were Christians and fine citizens.

This happened many years ago. It is now generally admitted that, from the Christian point of view, it was wrong for the Mennonites to resort to force. But some of us who have lived through those difficult years believe that here we can apply Christ's admonition, "Do not judge, so that you may not be judged" (Matt. 7:1).

It is also fitting for us to remember the tragic deaths of our brothers and sisters and the sorrow and tears of those who were left behind. To condemn and to judge would be quite shortsighted. Those people were no more guilty and possibly less guilty of injustice to peasants than you and me.

In retrospect, there are certain understandings to be gained from the fate of the Russian Mennonites. First, I think we can recognize that if these bandits had contented themselves with only robbery, few Mennonites would have resorted to force. Three factors are mainly accountable for the resistance offered: the cruel tortures, the ruthless murders, and the wholesale rape of old and young. These are the three things many Mennonite men simply found to be unbearable.

Another way of viewing the incident and accompanying reactions is to look at the history of nonresistance and to see these twentieth-century German-Russian Mennonites in their relationship to that history. For nearly four centuries, Mennonites had preached and taught nonresistance. Theoretically, people could become members of the Mennonite church only if through deep personal conviction they had accepted the faith as conceived by the Anabaptists. But practically, almost all the children born of Mennonite parents sooner or later did join the church of their forebears. This was true in Russia as in the other countries where the Mennonites lived.

As a result, the Mennonite congregations in Russia doubled in numbers about every twenty-five years. This was a tremendous increase. To teach these masses the original biblical beliefs of the Anabaptists was a gigantic task, not fully accomplished. Hence, there was a clash between theory and practice. The effect this clash had on the spiritual level of the churches may be part of the answer to this problem of apparent desertion of belief.

Then again, never in our recent history have such large numbers of our members been tested so fiercely and simultaneously. Surrounded by people of a different culture, flight was impossible. Imprisoned in their villages, they had to bear the full brunt of the test. Some remained loyal to the principle of nonresistance as practiced by the martyrs of the sixteenth century; others defended their family members when they were brutally attacked by the Makhno bands. What would you do?[40]

In Harmon, West Virginia, Richard Weaver engineered an amateur radio station, pictured here in 1949. By 1951 the Mennonite Church (MC) had established *The Mennonite Hour* broadcast in Harrisonburg, Virgina.

INSET Radios were forbidden in the Lancaster Conference, but Ada Leaman Leed sang the church's hymns over the airwaves.

The Bishops and the Nightingale

Alice W. Lapp

Not all Mennonite women in the 1930s stayed within their traditional roles. Some broke the mold. When radios were banned, one Lancaster County, Pennsylvania, woman not only listened to the radio, she also sang hymns on her own program. Since the story was first published, Ada Leaman Leed has died. Yet people are still inspired as they remember her cheerful attitude and her singing voice.

LIBERATED AND ASSERTIVE young women were not just a 1980s phenomenon. Many congregations include women who through the years did kingdom work in more than traditional housewifely roles.

One of these women, interviewed as a rosy-cheeked, ninety-two-year-old great-grandmother, was Ada Leaman Leed of Lancaster County, Pennsylvania. Ada sang hymns on her own weekly Lancaster radio program during the 1930s, when radios were forbidden by the Lancaster Mennonite Conference.

Born in 1893, Ada grew up in Lititz, Pennsylvania, and graduated from high school, continually developing her skills in both piano and voice. Frequently other churches invited her to sing solos, especially during summer vacations when their choirs were disbanded.

Ada also worked in the community as a canvassing volunteer. She worked ecumenically with church groups, organizing a variety of needlework projects around town and at Lancaster General Hospital. The children on the pediatrics ward listened to her lively reading of stories. This was long before television and radio provided entertainment for these little shut-ins.

In later years, Ada Leed lived in a pleasant, sunny cottage at Landis Homes near Lancaster, where she organized and sang in the Ladies' Choir. She beamed when she recalled that she always felt she was doing the Lord's work. In 1934, she began singing hymns in her own fifteen-minute radio program on WKJC in Lancaster, broadcasting from the Kirk Johnson Piano Store. Little did she dream that she was a pioneer for what later became nationwide and even international Mennonite radio ministries.

Her idea came as she listened to the radio and noticed that there were hardly any religious programs. First, she had to convince the station owners, who were certain no one would be interested. Soon her weekly *Morning Hymn Sing* began receiving dozens of letters with requests for "The Old Rugged Cross," "In the Garden," "Face to Face with Christ My Savior," and others. She usually sang accompanied by a friend on the piano or organ, but sometimes by herself.

In 1935, the station changed its call letters to WGAL and her program title to *The Friendly Singer*. Letters kept arriving from Conowingo to Willow Street, from Harrisburg to Lebanon, from Elizabethtown to New Holland. Many were from invalids who, in those early days of radio, relied on that medium for entertainment and inspiration.

In that period, Lancaster County Mennonite leadership considered radio "worldly" and banned it. So how did Ada get away with singing on the radio? One day a bishop from another district collared Jacob Hershey, the minister of the Lititz church, and demanded, "What are you going to do about Ada Leed? I understand that she is singing on the radio."

Hershey smiled as he replied, "She can sing as long as she likes. I won't do anything to stop her. She is doing the Lord's work."

Ada continued to broadcast until 1938, when she and her husband, with Orie and Elta Miller, sailed to Europe on the *Queen Mary* for a summer visit to possible Mennonite Central Committee locations. While they were gone, WGAL joined a national network, and sponsors were needed for what were now expensive time slots on the air. So that particular mission was ended.

Nevertheless, Ada kept lending her voice to community causes. Some said the congregational singing at the Lititz Mennonite Church has always seemed to "go better" when Ada was among the singers. The congregation voted her to be chorister at least three times during the 1940s. Each time the bishops sent the deacon to ask her to resign because they considered it unseemly for a woman to lead a mixed group.

She did form and lead a mixed chorus at Lititz in the 1960s. The group sang music by Alice Parker and other songs. Over a period of some thirty years, she also occasionally formed and directed ad hoc choirs for funerals at the church.

Ada did many things besides singing. She began attending the Lititz Mennonite congregation when it formed in 1906. In 1913, she married businessman Jacob Leed, became a member of the Mennonite Church after marriage, in the custom then. They soon began raising two sons and two daughters. A third daughter died after a childhood tonsillectomy. The other four children moved on to responsible professions and parenthood. In the 1980s, Ada was enjoying fourteen grandchildren and twelve great-grandchildren.

Along with her domestic duties, Ada made time to teach children's Sunday school classes. She said she was promoted through the years until she taught the elderly women of the church. Some of her former child pupils sat in the same older ladies' class with her. "Time does indeed level the ages," she said as her eyes twinkled.

How did Ada feel about the criticism that came her way? She shrugged it off and went on doing what she felt was God's will, supported by her husband and her minister. Never once did it occur to her to leave her denomination or even to change congregations. Ada Leed provides encouragement to young Mennonite entrepreneurs and others who have a mission to witness, however unusual or untraditional that mission might be.[41]

Mennonite General Conference, 1941, Kalona, Iowa: despite the pastoral setting, all was not well.

INSET Sanford C. Yoder, the voice of moderation, and the author, Edward Yoder.

A Soft Voice Speaking Truth Saves the Day

Edward Yoder

The 1930s and 1940s were difficult years in the Mennonite Church (MC). Leaders were faced by pressures of acculturation—language change from German to English and the erosion of the church's isolated rural character—and by the Fundamentalist-Modernist debate. In response, leaders sought to redefine a Mennonite identity. One solution was to emphasize "nonconformity to the world" in appearance and lifestyle by requiring uniformity to "plain" standards. In some district conferences, symbols of simplicity and moderation became tests of membership. Regional differences in defining and enforcing nonconformity threatened to divide the church, as this story shows.

———

A MOST SIGNIFICANT EVENT of 1944 was the special session of Mennonite General Conference (later Mennonite Church General Assembly), called as a last desperate effort to deal with the confusion, uncertainty, and distrust that had continued without resolution since the mid-1930s. The outcome of the carefully planned procedures of the 1944 sessions, under the leading of the Holy Spirit, was a dramatic climax of reconciliation that changed the character of Mennonite General Conference from that time on.

Although the conference was convened in the midst of doubts and questionings, the opening session on a Tuesday evening in August featured a keynote address on "Unity of the Spirit or Division," by John H. Mosemann. Newly elected moderator Allen Erb had envisioned this conference as a discussion on the polarities of legalism and libertinism, based on the books of Galatians and 1 Corinthians.

The conference devoted three sessions on Wednesday and two on Thursday for respected leaders to open topics and issues, followed by discussion and prayer. Before, after, and between official sessions, there were volunteer prayer meetings where conference participants learned to pray together and to know and respect each other.

On Thursday evening a 1943 report of the General Problems Committee, which had been given the task of promoting unity in doctrine and practice, was removed from the table. Instead, the session became an open discussion of a score of issues under the general umbrella of biblical interpretation, nonresistance, and nonconformity. Around these themes, the distrust of many years had been centered. In God's mysterious way, however, the Holy Spirit, through two days of official and voluntary sessions, had softened the hearts of many delegates; the time was ripe for the right person to speak words that could diffuse the tensions.

This person was sixty-four-year-old Sanford C. Yoder, who in 1940 had retired as president of Goshen College. Born near Kalona, Iowa, Sanford had been lured to the open ranges and cattle trails of the West. He was called back to the Midwest to serve as minister and bishop. In 1924 he reluctantly accepted the call to reopen and rebuild Goshen College. During the sixteen years of his presidency, he had silently suffered much as mediator between the established and sometimes reactionary church leaders and the emerging younger progressives who were his proteges.

In response to questions and statements as to the reason for the current distrust, Sanford quietly rose to the his full height of six feet and three inches; in his soft-spoken voice, he said in effect:

> You ask the reason for our situation? I'll tell you the reason. It is because fellowship has broken down. There was a time when we experienced the finest of Christian fellowship, but for some time this has no longer been possible. Today the feeling experienced is one of ostracism and division. The fellowship is gone. This is the reason for distrust and tension within the church.

When the speaker sat down, there was deathly silence. Had a pin been dropped, one could have heard it—until a brother suggested a time of prayer. After an hour of voluntary audible praying (one speaking at a time), the conference rose from its knees and resumed discussion.

There was more confession than discussion, however. One brother confessed that earlier in the conference, he had spoken unkind words against Sanford Yoder; now he was asking forgiveness. Another confessed that he had come to the conference thinking they might as well divide; he asked to be forgiven for that attitude. More confession and reconciliation followed.

As the meeting drew to a close, it was announced that the Friday morning session would be receiving a report from the Resolutions Committee, followed by action on the 1943 report of the General Problems Committee. Following the benediction, a brother said to me, "Whatever is done tomorrow will have little meaning. The purpose of the special session of General Conference was achieved this evening." The brother was right. The dramatic evening session had given birth to a new Mennonite General Conference. The old had died. The new was born in 1944.[42]

Seeking another home: Mennonite refugees boarding the
SS *Charlton Monarch*, bound for Paraguay, May 16, 1948.

INSET Trust restored: Joop (alias Heinz Wiebe), Anneke, and
Wiebe Postma.

A Mennonite Imposter

Peter J. Dyck

The stories of Peter and Elfrieda Dyck are well known throughout the world. After World War II, they served in Europe under Mennonite Central Committee, coordinating relief efforts and the migration of Mennonite refugees to Canada and Paraguay. In this unusual story, a man pretending to be a Prussian Mennonite refugee outfoxes Peter Dyck. Peter's candid story ends with the impostor's confession and the reconciliation of their relationship. Only Peter can tell a story like this.

As HE STOOD there before me in the office in Gronau, Germany, in 1946, it was immediately clear that he was not a typical Mennonite refugee. There was something about his bearing, his self-assurance, and even his handshake that instantly set him apart from the other refugees from Russia. Then he spoke, not in low German as was their custom, but in high German, a flawless high German.

He didn't even pretend to be a Russian Mennonite. He said he was a Prussian, single, and a teacher by profession. But like so many others, he was a refugee and wanted to go to Paraguay. He said his name was Heinz Wiebe.

"Why go with the Russian Mennonites?" I asked. I pointed out that later there probably would be a transport for his own Prussian people, though at the time MCC didn't know when that would be or to which overseas country.

"I don't want to wait," he said. "I love the Russian Mennonites. Furthermore, in Paraguay they will need teachers, and I am a teacher. I know taking me along would be an exception," he added understandingly, "but why can't MCC make one exception?"

I didn't promise. Instead, I asked C. F. Klassen, the MCC director, to interview Heinz Wiebe. C. F., as we called my brother-in-law, didn't have time; he assured me that whatever my decision, he would support it. "You interview and screen thousands of refugees," he said. "Your judgment is as good as mine."

I was impressed with Heinz Wiebe during our second interview. The man had gifts and a good education. He certainly would be an asset to any community of pioneers struggling to put their lives together in Paraguay. As he left the office, he thanked me for accepting him into the Russian Mennonite transport for Paraguay.

He happened to land on the third of the MCC chartered ships, the ill-fated *Charlton Monarch*, which never reached its destination. Elfrieda, my wife, was the only MCC escort on this unhappy ship, with its bad engines and rotten crew. Later, she told me again and again how helpful Heinz Wiebe had been in those indescribably difficult days and weeks on the high seas.

Soon after the *Charlton Monarch* had left Bremerhaven in Germany on May 16, 1948, with 758 passengers on board, I took a trainload of refugees to Rotterdam, Holland, for immigration to Canada. On arrival there, a Dutch lady asked to speak with me. I was busy with embarking details, but she waited patiently most of the day until the ship had left.

I apologized for keeping her waiting so long and was even more sorry when I heard what her request was. She wanted MCC to take her, a citizen of Holland and a Mennonite, along on one of its refugee transports to South America. "If I had known your request, I could have told you right away when we met in the morning that the answer is no," I explained. "MCC is moving refugees only; we are not transporting normal passengers, people like you."

With a faint smile momentarily gliding over her attractive face, she said, "Since you took my husband, I thought you might also take me to Paraguay."

The next hour must have been torture for the poor woman. I learned that her surname name was Postma, and I assured her that we had not taken any man by that name to Paraguay. She admitted that her husband had gone under an assumed name but would not reveal it. "That would be betraying him," she said. I remember getting up as if to go when she anxiously asked what I planned to do.

"Nothing at all," I replied. Then I added that perhaps back in Germany, I'd tell my co-workers in the refugee camp that I had met a woman in Holland who told me a strange and incredible story. It was about a husband and a ship and Paraguay—and not a word of it was true. "But it's all true," she insisted, with tears welling up in her blue eyes.

For the umpteenth time, I insisted that unless and until she revealed the assumed name of her alleged husband, I would not and could not help her.

By that time we were sitting in the MCC car and I was ready to leave. She had turned pale, and I noticed beads of perspiration on her forehead. I was sorry for the poor woman, but what could I do? Her hands trembled as she slowly opened her purse. She pulled out a small picture and handed it to me without a word.

"Heinz Wiebe!" I gasped in surprise. She was crying when I handed the picture back to her. "Please," she said, "please take me to Paraguay to my husband." I was stunned.

Driving back to Germany, I had lots of time to think about this strange and cruel twist of events and to think about the sudden revelation. So that smart-looking Prussian was in reality a Dutchman, the handsome single fellow was a married man with a wife and two children, and the teacher was really a minister. How cleverly he had pulled the wool over my eyes. But why? What would C. F. Klassen say when he found out how I'd been fooled? I should have insisted that *he* interview this so-called Heinz Wiebe. I wondered whether he would have been able to peel back the Heinz Wiebe layers and discover the real Joop (YOPE) Postma hiding inside.

By the time he arrived in Paraguay, the police were already looking for him. That was not our plan, but a series of muddled communications had triggered the manhunt. Heinz Wiebe disappeared.

In October of that year, Elfrieda and I took the fourth MCC transport of 1,693 refugees to South America. We had barely arrived at the MCC office in Asuncion, Paraguay, when the telephone rang. It was Heinz Wiebe. The MCC staff was excited and baffled. How did he know we were there? Where was he?

I can still see him coming up the path a day or two later, to the secret rendezvous we had agreed upon. There was the knock on the door. Then Heinz Wiebe stood facing Elfrieda and me.

We wondered how this meeting would turn out, realizing that much depended on how it would start. I was prepared for almost any kind of opening, from hearing his lame excuses to frank confessions. But I was not prepared for what followed.

I had remembered the man who had lied to me as being handsome, gifted, and possessing leadership qualities, but I had forgotten that he was also a bit of a charmer, with all the traits of a gentleman. Turning first to the lady, Heinz Wiebe reached for Elfrieda's hand, bowed low, kissed it, and in the best European style introduced himself as "Joop Postma."

While I had met him only during the interviews, Elfrieda had spent almost eight weeks with him on board ship. In many ways Heinz Wiebe had been most helpful. He was one of her trusted staff, and he certainly knew how to inspire the young people. So when he now solemnly revealed his true identity and so seriously announced that his name was Joop Postma, Elfrieda burst out laughing. The whole thing suddenly struck her as extremely funny.

After that, Heinz Wiebe was dead and Joop Postma was very much alive. He became active in school and church in Paraguay and Brazil. His good wife and children ultimately joined him. He went about confessing and apologizing in person in South America and by letter in North America. An MCC minute of August 29, 1956, notes that a letter had been received from J. S. Postma "asking forgiveness of the MCC for his transgression against MCC in 1948." The minute concludes by stating that it was "moved and passed that we forgive Brother Postma." He also wrote to me and I replied that it was okay, he had not hurt me or damaged my reputation.

Nine years later we met again. It was at the Mennonite World Conference in Karlsruhe, Germany, in 1957. He told Elfrieda and me how everyone in Paraguay, in Brazil, in Germany, and also in the MCC had forgiven him. "Only you have not forgiven me," he said, looking straight at me.

This time Elfrieda did not laugh. We talked for a long time. I told him again that everything was okay, I had forgiven him. He asked whether I trusted him. There was a long silence. I said no. For me, there was a big difference between forgiving him and trusting him.

The man was clever. Ten years earlier Europe had burned under his feet because Nazis and Nazi-sympathizers were rounded up and brought to trial. Although he was innocent, his cultural affiliations with Germans made him suspect. So he wanted out. A bit of fibbing in my office had done the trick. Now he wanted to come back in again, into the fold of the Mennonite brotherhood, symbolized by the Mennonite World Conference in session at that very moment. So this time he again got his way by going around with confessions. Did I trust him? No!

Perhaps for the first time, I began seriously to examine

my attitude toward Joop Postma. What I discovered bothered me. I was like the early Christians who remained aloof from Paul because they continued to see Saul in him (Acts 9:26). They did not trust him.

The following day we met again, Joop and Anneke—his ever-so-faithful wife—with Elfrieda and me. We drank a lot of tea. In the end we shook hands as brothers and went to communion together, a meaningful and memorable communion. As far as I was concerned, this time it was settled—settled between me and Joop and settled also between me and the Lord.

Not many months later, I received a letter from him inviting me to hold a series of meetings in his church in Holland. Before looking at my calendar to see whether the suggested dates were open, I knew that I would say yes. This would have priority. I would have to go. I wanted to go.

We were gathered at his church for the last meeting of the week. It was the night for young people, and we were nearing the end of the question-and-answer period. Suddenly my friend and their pastor, Joop Postma, was on his feet, thanking me for having come and telling these teenagers all about that murky incident years ago when he had lied to me. "Don't do that," I whispered to him as urgently as possible. "That's just between us and the Lord."

He pushed me gently aside and continued sharing with the young people, not sparing himself, but telling it exactly the way it had been. The breathless silence was only interrupted by an occasional sob from one of the young people as they listened to the confessions of their pastor and witnessed the overpowering grace of God. As he put his arms around me, he asked the young people to take a good look at the two of us, because what they were witnessing here was confession and forgiveness, reconciliation and peace, the kind that only the Spirit of God could bring about.

The next year our family moved into the Postma residence for one of the most relaxed and happy vacations of our ten years in Europe, while the Postma family spent their vacation in Germany. With them was their youngest child, a son, born in Paraguay, who has the unusual name of "Wiebe."[43]

A new home built in the rubble of Bremen, Germany, during World War II.

INSET Songs died away: Mennonite refugees trekking west from Russia, about 1943.

Escape from Communism

Johann D. Rempel

*When many Russian Mennonites emigrated from Russia
in the 1870s and the 1920s, a significant number
remained. The turmoil of World War II caused another
exodus of German-speaking Russians. Those who were
overtaken by the Communist army were "repatriated"
and sent to slave labor camps in Siberia. Many others
were killed in bombing raids on cities where they sought
refuge. This is the story of the Rempel family, who
against many odds, succeeded in escaping to the West in
the 1940s. Readers also need to remember that the same
German government and military that protected these
Russian Mennonites was responsible for killing millions
of Jews and other victims. Some Mennonites, sadly,
likely cooperated in such crimes.*

———

THE RETREAT OF the German army from Russia in 1943
signified the exodus for many German-speaking
Russians, including Mennonites. This meant bidding
farewell to our homes and abandoning the family thresholds
that our ancestors had established nearly 150 years earlier.
We saw portents of this destiny; it had to come, and it came
sooner than many expected.

Soon we would have to leave our homes, gardens, and
farmyards. We would have to journey to distant lands and
part from our meadows, fields, valleys, and the old Dnieper

113

River—never to meet again. On the other hand, we might remain and later be sent to the frigid land of Siberia, where we would likely suffer unbearable tortures; most would succumb to the frightfulness of the persecutors.

The people of Old Colony (Chortitza) will never forget September 1943. It was a severe, unmerciful month, sorely wounding the spirits of many fathers and mothers and robbing them forever of all enthusiasm for life. The last days of September were filled with preparation: clothes, kitchen utensils, and precious belongings were packed in trunks. All were to be transported into Germany.

We loaded our baggage on the train and spent our first night at the railway, awaiting our departure. On the night of September 29, we left. The train of thirty cars was carrying 997 persons. The evening before, I had gone the length of the train, looking for relatives. The people stood at the open doors of the cars, gazing for the last time upon Einlage. Many could not restrain their tears. Some began to sing, but the songs died away.

Only on the third day were we told that our train was destined for Lodz (Litzmannstadt), Poland. We were given food and drink. The crowded cars, with thirty persons in each plus baggage, made traveling especially burdensome. There was no chance to recline for rest or sleep.

After delousing operations at Lodz, we continued to Danzig, arriving there on October 10, 1943. Our train passed through the city, arriving at Neustadt two hours later. At last we had reached a resettlement camp. It was composed of ten barracks in addition to a kitchen, a hospital, a headquarters building, two laundry and bath houses, and a kindergarten.

The administrator and his assistants took us into custody. Our baggage remained in the cars. We took up quarters and organized our camp group. Eight to ten persons occupied each room of about nineteen by thirteen feet. We piled our belongings near and under the beds.

The administrator acquainted us with the rules of camp life. A barbed-wire fence about sixteen or eighteen feet high enclosed the whole camp. No one was to leave camp. Meals were to be prepared in the kitchen and could then be taken to the barracks. Every barrack was to select a leader to assist in the program of camp administration.

Soon a school was opened; I and the five other teachers from Einlage could again teach the children. While much was still wanting and we were very crowded, we could still exercise our profession. Many refugees found employment in the factories of the city. However, they could not quiet their feelings of homesickness; throughout the camp, the old home in Einlage continued to be the subject of conversation.

A train with seventy officials was stationed at the depot. We were all questioned as to name, parents, grandparents, and other relatives. We were given medical examinations. At the conclusion of this process, we received our *Deutsche Ausweise* (German documents). We were now *Reichsdeutsche* (German citizens) rather than just *Volksdeutsche* (ethnic Germans).

As citizens of Germany, we were expected to undertake responsibilities and accept work assigned to us. I was assigned as teacher at the municipal girls' school; other teachers were assigned to the villages. Several hundred were taken to the Speers armament works of Dresden; others were taken to Zoppot and Danzig. The youth were mobilized into the armed forces.

The group transported to Dresden met with much misfortune. In Dresden their quarters consisted of an old granary without windows or doors. Their baggage did not follow. They were forced to build quarters of their own in the forests. In the fall of 1944, a group from the resettlement camp was taken to the Warthegau, where they became victims of the Red (Communist) army. Most of these people were sent to Siberia.

Thus the people of Einlage were torn asunder, never again

to meet one another. Many lost their lives; others, as seen above, were "repatriated"; others eventually came to Paraguay and Canada; some remained in Germany.

Only eight Einlage families remained in camp, but soon a transport of *Wosnesener* (Ascensionists, likely Adventists) arrived from the Dniester (Moldavia/Moldova) region. These refugees again filled the barracks. At night millions of bedbugs found their way through crevices in the walls and plagued the people. Many tried to close the crevices, others tried various powders. All was in vain. The children cried, and the mothers despaired. We spread our straw mattresses upon the floor and poured water on them, for some measure of protection. I spent many a night out of doors.

Thus we lived in the camp until January 1945. Humans soon learn to adjust to even the worst living conditions. The situation at the front was deteriorating rapidly. The people became more restless and the Poles more arrogant because of the ill treatment they had received from the Germans. In the camp we sensed that we would have to prepare for a second flight.

One day the camp officer announced to the camp inmates: "All who have relatives and friends in Germany, shall have their official papers prepared at once, as it is dangerous to remain longer in camp." Again possessions were abandoned, and we took along only necessary clothes, linens, and bedding. The station was already crowded with refugees from the city and vicinity.

With some pushing, we succeeded in boarding a construction train going directly to Dresden, also our destination. Since we found ourselves in a warehouse car, we found sitting room only on oil drums, bars, or other equipment. In this cold, drafty, and filthy car, we rode five days and five nights. The express passenger train covers this distance in eight hours. Snow entered through the sagging doors, and the extreme cold threatened to freeze hands and feet.

In Berlin we stopped for a night, where we suffered

through an air raid. It was a terrifying night, ruled by the powers of darkness. Blessedly, we were unhurt. When the air had cleared in the morning, we continued on our way, finally arriving in Dresden.

I had read and heard much of Dresden as the city of art and culture. I now utilized all my free time to personally see all places of importance. Daily I wandered through the streets and saw the opera house, the theatre, the Zwinger Museum, the famous Frauenkirche, the royal palace, and many other buildings.

On the night of January 13, 1945, Dresden experienced its first air raid, followed the next day by several more raids. Then Dresden lay in dust and ashes, a second Sodom and Gomorrah. The terrible scenes of destruction were indescribable. For two weeks the fires raged. At the railroad station, five thousand refugees lost their lives. Soon the air was filled with the odor of two hundred thousand partly burned corpses. Those still living made such a wretched picture of weeping and lamentation.

On March 30, 1945, we left Dresden for Bernsdorf. However, the roar of the Russian cannon gave us no rest, and we were forced also to leave this place. On April 14 our daughter Martha and her husband, Peter, left us with a group and went west. The next evening our daughter Marie, my wife and I, and the family of Jakob Rempel left Bernsdorf with our possessions in two small wagons. For days and nights, we trudged westward through rain and mist. The roar of cannon followed us. We rested in hay fields, barns, and ravines.

Since the bridge in Pirna was bombed out, we followed the traffic north of Pirna, where we found a variegated mass of refugees with horse-drawn carts and hand wagons. Many were on foot. All wanted to cross the river. With some pushing, we succeeded in crossing. Wet, hungry, tired, and discouraged, we stood at the crossroads in Heidenau. Where to now?

Marie and others went into the city to find room. Refusal followed refusal until the wife of a soldier allowed us to use a room and the kitchen. Soon we were again expected to move, but I was tired and sickly. The parents of the soldier's wife offered us quarters. We were given ration cards and thus settled down for a more extended stay. In spite of the Russian victories, we remained, trusting our destiny to the Lord. On May 9, 1945, the Russians arrived. To describe the events of the next three days would require a ream of paper and two weeks' time.

On May 15, 1945, I was called to the city hall. The mayor and his assistants, fifteen men in all, wanted to learn the Russian language. Within a week, a second study group was formed, and soon a third. On June 1, the course opened with thirty-eight students. Again I was a teacher. Every day I instructed attentive students for two or three hours. Marie became official translator for the police in Nieder-Sedlitz, the industrial suburban area of Dresden. A total of eighty-three took instruction in Russian, including teachers, officials, doctors, musicians, and actors.

After a separation of eight months, we received our first letter from Martha, now in the western zone. On the evening of the same day, I received an official notice: "All Russo-Germans must be taken back [to Russia]." Through my urgent pleading and with the support of my physician, I was allowed stay. I continued to teach Russian in the eighth and ninth grades. We prepared to celebrate Christmas in the family circle. But again the order came for us to be taken back.

We took refuge in flight. After several temporary residences, we located in Nieder-Sedlitz. Again I was asked to instruct the officials in the city hall in the Russian language. Soon I was also recognized as official translator. In reality I was now serving two masters. Anxiety for the future occupied us at all times. At different occasions Marie was asked to report to the Russian authorities.

We felt clearly that our safety depended upon our further

change of residence to a more secure area. Our daughter Martha, from whom we had been separated for over a year, invited us to come to the British zone. After being notified by the chief of police to appear before the Russian authorities, we felt the time for action had come. We decided to prepare the necessary papers and leave. The mayor and his force were reluctant to see us depart since we were their chief liaison agents with the Russian authorities. Finally, however, we received our dismissal, and Mother packed our things for another flight.

As darkness fell on the night of June 7, 1946, I again retired to my usual place of security in the garden. The new day dawned, and I awoke Mother and Marie. We took our farewell and went to the depot. After boarding the train, we left the Russian zone, where we had lived for fourteen months in anxious insecurity. We arrived at the zonal boundary on Pentecost. The various inspections consumed several days. We found several thousand refugees from the Russian zone.

On the evening of June 12, we were met by our children Martha and Peter. It was a joyful reunion. At last we were in safety, unlike many thousands who had been "repatriated" by the Russians and sent to slave labor camps in Siberia.[44]

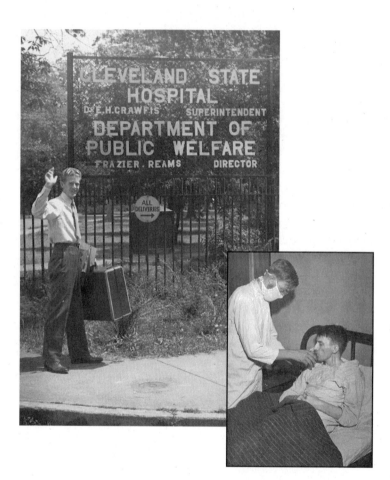

Reporting for active duty in the war against the causes of mental illness, 1945.

INSET Civilian Public Service accepts an obligation to improve the deplorable conditions of the mentally ill.

Doing Good in Wartime

Grant M. Stoltzfus

*During World War II, conscientious objectors worked
on farms, did conservation work, fought forest fires,
served as human guinea pigs for medical research, and
worked in mental hospitals. Those who were assigned
to mental hospitals found mental health care to be primitive and inadequate. Following their service experience,
many Mennonite young men studied medicine and
founded a mental health care movement. As a result of
doing good in a time of war, mental health care
improved dramatically.*

PERHAPS IT WAS not altogether by accident that conscientious objectors served in mental hospitals during World
War II. To those who served, it became clear that mental illness, like war itself, is "a symptom of the deadly degeneracy
of our civilization." It was a good thing for those who could
not wage war to learn firsthand about some of the things
that make for war.

A combination of circumstances brought conscientious
objectors to about one-fifth of the nation's three hundred
public mental institutions during World War II. The war
boom in industry caused a critical labor shortage on hospital
staffs. There were also several thousand young men in the
base camps with a desire to do other service, perhaps something more closely related to human suffering and need.

The demand and the supply would not have met if the church agencies operating Civilian Public Service (CPS)— American Friends Service Committee, Brethren Service Committee, and Mennonite Central Committee—had not worked patiently under the Selective Service System to make mental hospital service an actuality. The Friends opened the first unit at Williamsburg, Virginia, in mid-1942. The first Mennonite Central Committee unit was opened on September 11, 1942, at Staunton, Virginia.

In all, about sixty institutions were staffed in part by CPS men. About half of the strength of the CPS hospital units was made up of men from the Mennonite base camps. Approximately 1,400 men served in Mennonite Central Committee hospital units at some time during their CPS experience.

For most men in hospital units, the duties were those of ordinary ward attendants. Bathing, feeding, and caring for the patients became the daily routine. Some men worked in therapy departments, some in kitchens, and a few on the farms. Work hours were usually long, some even exceeding sixty or seventy-two hours per week. Each man received an allowance of fifteen dollars per month.

The men lived as regular employees in the dormitories and were usually permitted to live with their wives when they were also employed by the institution. Each unit had its leader, a CPS man. The larger units, with up to a hundred men, also were staffed with an educational director. These leaders arranged for religious and social programs, and offered the men courses in Bible, psychiatry, and other fields. Occasional conferences and visits by ministers, Mennonite Central Committee officials, and representatives of the colleges brought encouragement and vision to the men.

Most CPSers did good work in mental hospitals. There were sad exceptions where men failed to give their best and took a negative attitude toward the opportunity to witness and serve. Not all persons can adapt to the exacting duties of caring for the mentally ill.

The extent of mental illness impressed itself on the men in the units: seven hundred thousand people were in mental hospitals, and perhaps many times that number were suffering from forms of mental illness. One person out of twenty spent some time in a mental hospital. One out of ten needed treatment at some time for mental illness. One family in five suffered from mental illness. Nor had the war decreased the number of mental sufferers.

In addition to grasping the scope of mental derangement, CPSers came to see something even more depressing. All too often, society has overlooked the plight of its mental victims. Many state hospitals, the conscientious objectors found, were "hospitals" only by courtesy of name. The level and care of treatment was found to be inferior—even shockingly poor.

First, the CPSers found overcrowded wards, ill-prepared food, filthy floors, and shoddy clothing. Second, they observed low-paid attendants, understaffed institutions, and lack of medical care. These all combined to make the institutions anything but restorative to their patients. The CPSers discovered that such conditions were general, not just local or characteristic of any one state.

Men who wanted to do work of national importance were not denied the opportunity in the mental hospitals and training schools. In each unit were some men who had the vision and courage to try new and better things in behalf of the patients. More frequent baths, more recreation, gentle instead of rough handling—these were tried and with good results.

CPS men started a Mental Hygiene Program in a unit at Philadelphia. They published *The Attendant,* a periodical for workers in mental institutions; wrote handbooks for attendants; and did legal research. An important feature of this program was contacting the men in the different units and collecting data and statements about their institutions.

The Mennonite units joined in the Mental Hygiene Program. They wrote handbook articles and pamphlets, aided in briefing state mental health laws, recorded their experiences in the files of the program, and participated in conferences. When the Selective Service System permitted the staff of the Mental Hygiene Program to be enlarged, two men from Mennonite Central Committee units were chosen to work in the Mental Hygiene Program Educational Division.

Out of this movement, born of CPS, has grown the National Mental Health Foundation, sponsored by leading citizens, and "dedicated to the conservation of mental health and to the highest attainable standards of treatment and care for the mentally ill and mentally deficient." Through magazines, press, radio, and movies, the Foundation has launched a public educational program. By way of publications and legal research, it has helped institutions and legislatures to meet the problem of mental illness.

One CPSer reflected on his experience:

Since working in a mental institution, I feel an obligation to the community when I return home after the war. Since learning the various causes which place people in these institutions, I feel it is my duty to correct these conditions. I see the need of a higher standard for well-balanced moral and Christian living. I feel we should provide similar institutions for our own people.

The sentiment of the CPS man who wrote these words has come to be shared by others. A survey of Mennonite congregations reveals a sizable quota of mentally ill and mentally deficient persons. If the Mennonite churches should ever decide [as they later did[45]] to establish a mental hospital or to continue service to the mentally ill through service units and otherwise, there is no doubt that the hospital experience of CPS would furnish an excellent foundation.

Referring to the CPS Units, Dr. George S. Stevenson, of the National Committee for Mental Hygiene, remarked that the loss of a few thousand men from the armed forces is a small price for the country to pay to have within its mental institutions young men with the ideals and talents for a program of better care. Dr. Earl Bond, a former president of the American Psychiatry Association, told Selective Service officials that such opportunities as CPS represented come "once in a century."

One superintendent from an eastern institution wrote regarding the unit in his hospital: "It is impossible to see how the hospital could have functioned had it not been for the assistance of men assigned in the Civilian Public Service Unit."

The director of a midwestern state's public welfare department said in a letter to the Mennonite Central Committee:

> Your men and women all served faithfully, and helped us to care more adequately for their [institution's] mentally ill and mentally deficient during the war period. I should like to take this opportunity to thank each individual member of the camps in this state, as well as the men who came from the central office to organize the work and plan with us.

What kind of a world produces so many mental breakdowns? Is it not a world of much competition—social, economic, and political? Is it not a world of racial discrimination, economic injustice, and class conflict? Is it not a world that has turned its back on moral law and has wreaked great havoc on the home? Is it not a world that has enthroned values that contradict the central emphasis of the Christian faith as interpreted by Mennonites for generations?

What kind of a society fails to care for its mental victims and to prevent their increase? Is it not one that lacks the ability to face fear and conflict? Is it not a world that feeds on suspicion and stale delusions? Finally, is it not a world that rejects the self-giving love of the Christ who preached and lived out the Sermon on the Mount?

The challenge has come to us to learn from mental victims. The challenge comes to declare war against the sins that make people, often through no fault of their own, the victims of mental instability. The challenge comes to bring a Christian ministry to those with bewildered minds. Any group that testifies to a Christ who desires that we love and understand each other *always* can be a blessing to the mentally handicapped.[46]

THE ANABAPTIST VISION

Harold S. Bender

"Judged by the reception it met at the hands of those in power, both
in Church and State, equally in Roman Catholic and in Protestant countries,
the Anabaptist movement was one of the most tragic in the history of
Christianity; but, judged by the principles which were put into play by
the men who bore this reproachful nickname, it must be pronounced one of
the most momentous and significant undertakings in man's eventful religious
struggle after the truth. It gathered up the gains of earlier movements,
and it is the spiritual soil out of which all nonconformist sects have
sprung, and it is the first plain announcement in modern history of a pro-
gramme for a new type of Christian society which the modern world, especially
in America and England, has been slowly realizing--an absolutely free and
independent religious society, and a State in which every man counts as a
man, and has his share in shaping both Church and State."

These words of Rufus M. Jones① constitute one of the best character-
izations of Anabaptism and its contribution to our modern Christian culture
to be found in the English language. They were brave words when they were
written thirty-five years ago, but they have been abundantly verified
by a generation of Anabaptist research since that time.② There can be no
question but that the great principles of freedom of conscience, separation of church and state, and voluntaris

Protestantism, and so essential to democr

the Anabaptists of the Reformation perio

enunciated them, and challenged the Chri

tice. The line of descent through the c

Manuscript of the speech: a usable and respectable history.

INSET Harold S. Bender: he did not know he had produced a
classic.

Presenting the Anabaptist Vision

Albert N. Keim

The Anabaptist Vision is legendary among North American Mennonites, as is its author, Harold S. Bender (1897-1962). The Vision gave Mennonites a respectable history and a useful theology during a time of crisis. For all its formative influence, its creation and delivery were a small detail in Bender's frenetic schedule. Albert Keim, who has since written a major biography of Bender, describes the creation and presentation of the speech, which was later printed and read widely.

A S THE STOUT black-clad chairman opened the meeting with a brisk prayer, he had the appearance of a middle-aged priest. His receding hairline, dark eyes, strong nose, and a mouth that smiled easily conveyed a sense of congenial intelligence, the personality of a good parish priest. But the coat was Mennonite, and its wearer was Harold S. Bender, dean and acting president of Goshen College. At that moment he was the presiding president of the fifty-fifth meeting of the American Society of Church History.

The place of the meeting was Room 104 in Milbank Chapel, at Columbia University in New York City. It was 3:20 in the afternoon on Tuesday, December 28, 1943. The meeting began twenty minutes late because the train Bender took from Indiana arrived late in New York, not an unusual occurrence under the conditions of wartime transportation. Travel during that week after Christmas was even worse than usual because the railroad unions were threatening to strike for higher overtime pay.

By the time Harold arrived in New York City, President Franklin D. Roosevelt had ordered the army to take over the railroads. There would be no strike. Actually, Bender was fortunate to be at the meeting. It was only at the last minute that a Pullman berth became available, making possible his twenty-hour rail journey to New York.

As presiding officer, Bender's first order of business was the sad announcement of the death of Dr. Thomas Clinton Pears Jr., just forty-eight hours earlier. Pears, from Philadelphia, had been the longtime secretary of the society. The twenty-five members present elected Professor Matthew Spinka to be acting secretary.

After several other items of business, two papers were read. The most engaging paper was by David M. Cory on "The Religious History of the Mohawk and Oneida Tribes of the Iroquois Confederacy." Interspersed during the reading of the paper were a number of songs in the Iroquois language, sung by two members of the Iroquois tribe. It provided a colorful accent to the otherwise decorous proceedings of the society meeting.

At seven o'clock the Society held its annual dinner at the Columbia University Men's Faculty Club. The address of the outgoing president of the society followed the dinner. Harold Bender entitled his address, "The Anabaptist Vision." The thirty-minute speech was followed by what the minutes described as "a very lively discussion which would have undoubtedly continued much longer were it not for lack of time, for President Bender had to leave soon afterwards by plane to attend a meeting in Chicago."[47]

As president, Bender also chaired the Council of the American Society of Church History. The council was the

governing body of the church history society. At the conclusion of the presidential address, the council retired to one of
the Men's Faculty Club chambers for their annual meeting.
Bender presided. Only six of the ten members of the council
were present.

Acting secretary Spinka reported that during the year
membership had declined slightly. Total membership was
369, including Mennonites Cornelius Krahn, C. Henry
Smith, and Harold's two colleagues on the *Mennonite
Quarterly Review* editorial board, Robert Friedmann and
Ernst Correll. The previous year John C. Wenger had
resigned his membership; Guy Hershberger had been
dropped from the rolls for failure to pay society dues.

New council members were elected, Harold being one of
them. He was also appointed chair of the committee on program and local arrangements for the 1944 meeting in
Chicago. The other members of his committee were
University of Chicago Professors Sidney Mead and Wilhelm
Pauck. In his last action as president, Bender appointed his
friend Roland Bainton to preside at the meeting of the society the next day.

That done, he caught a taxi to LaGuardia Field and
boarded a plane for Cleveland, where sometime after midnight he caught the train to Chicago. At 12:30, just after
lunch, he was at his place as secretary of the executive committee of Mennonite Central Committee (MCC) in one of
the conference rooms at the Atlantic Hotel, ready for a day
and a half of intense meetings dealing with the burgeoning
Civilian Public Service (CPS) program.[48]

In the busy, hectic life of Harold Bender in 1943, the
forty-two-hour dash to New York City was a minor episode.
During the fall of 1943, he served as acting president of
Goshen College in addition to being dean while the president
of the college, Ernest Miller, attended Princeton Seminary.

As chair of the Mennonite Peace Problems Committee, he
was preoccupied with growing criticism coming from con-

servatives in the church regarding the CPS program. He was also in charge of the educational program at the CPS camps, which required frequent travel to CPS locations. As secretary of MCC, he carried on a huge correspondence. He was also editor of the *Mennonite Quarterly Review.* Somehow he also found time to teach two courses.

In the midst of such a maelstrom of activity, it is no wonder that Bender was able to give little time to the writing of "The Anabaptist Vision." As late as December 16, less than two weeks before he was to give it, he had not written it.[49] When he finally got to the writing, he wrote it in just a few days. His wife, Elizabeth Horsch Bender, remembered that she "was just amazed how he got that whole thing done and ready to give . . . in no time at all: two or three days."[50]

In the rush of preparation, he did not take time to do the careful source citations the essay required. Because the annual presidential address was to be published in *Church History,*[51] Bender had to go back and insert the necessary research apparatus. Sometime in January 1944, a Goshen College student saw Harold and Elizabeth and John C. Wenger sitting at the long table in the Historical Library at the college, surrounded by great mounds of books, intently searching for references. The student remembered John C. Wenger's gleeful chuckle as he announced, "I've found another one."[52] They were busy preparing "The Anabaptist Vision" for publication.

Thus Harold Bender created the classic and seminal essay in Mennonite history. The speech was written in haste, read to a tiny audience of less than twenty academicians, none of whom were Mennonite, in a richly paneled dining room at an Ivy League University in the heart of New York City. Bender could not have imagined what his presidential address would ultimately become.

Bender also could not have guessed how powerful an influence "The Anabaptist Vision" would be, both on the world of Anabaptist scholarship and on the self-understanding of his own people, the Mennonites. He did not know that he had produced a classic, promptly published as a booklet, *The Anabaptist Vision,* that is still in print.[53]

Spirited singing and direct preaching: "The Whole Gospel for the Whole World," Goshen, Indiana, early 1950s.

INSET The Brunk brothers: George, the preacher, and Lawrence, the song leader, 1951.

Revive Us Again: Brunk Brothers Tent Revivals

Ford Berg

Beginning in 1951, tent revivals made a huge impact on many Mennonite communities, from Florida to British Columbia. While the charismatic Brunk brothers, Lawrence and George R. II, led the way, others such as Howard Hammer, Andrew Jantzi, and Myron Augsburger followed. These Mennonite evangelists, while borrowing the medium from Protestant revivalism, shaped the content to include such Mennonite themes as discipleship, nonresistance, and nonconformity to the world. Some objected to the emotionalism of mass revivalism, while many others, like the nicknamed Franconia Cowboys, gave fervent testimonies and demonstrated changed lives. The writer presents a favorable picture of the first campaign in Lancaster, Pennsylvania.

THE BRUNK BROTHERS, Lawrence and George, pitched a tent seating 2,500 people in Lancaster, Pennsylvania, on June 4, 1951. Soon a second tent was added, but still these tents could not hold the crowds.

Each night crowds came and the tents overflowed. After five weeks the tents were moved to an airport on the edge of the city. Attendance reached a peak of 17,000 on the final

Sunday evening, July 22, seven weeks after the meetings began. Lancaster County had never seen anything like this.

More than 1,500 people, mostly Mennonites of the Lancaster area, signed decision cards, although additional thousands were stirred as a result of the revival meetings. An outward indication of the effectiveness of the meetings was demonstrated by Mennonite farmers who plowed up their fields of tobacco. Others threw cigarettes, pipes, whiskey, playing cards, jewelry, and other items that they felt had been a hindrance to their lives, into an offering rack marked "Offering for Baal."

Because revivals cannot possibly be measured by numbers, the real and total effect in the Lancaster area is unknown. That it is great is certain. Several thousand in the community were saved or restored. Many, it is reported, were living lives of formality, with little apparent understanding and appreciation for the true gospel of Christ.

Maurice E. Lehman, one of the ministers of the East Chestnut Street Mennonite Church, which sponsored the campaign, reported in the September 4, 1951, *Gospel Herald:*

> The evangelist preached against sin for many nights at the beginning of the revival. This preaching brought conviction of hidden sin of the flesh and spirit. Many church members confessed sin and "got right" with God. Brother George Brunk made the statement that this is a cleanup program as well as an evangelistic campaign. . . . We who have witnessed this great revival can say we will long remember it as one of the greatest events in our day.

From Lancaster the Brunk brothers moved their equipment to the Franconia Conference, north of Philadelphia. A huge tent, with a seating capacity of six thousand, was set up toward the last of the campaign. The work was supported by all of the bishops of the conference and almost all the ministers and deacons.

As at Lancaster, interest was great from the beginning. The crowds ranged from 2,500 on Monday and Friday evenings to 10-12,000 on Sunday evenings. Admittedly, the large crowds were not the heart of the revival but rather the personal lives changed and committed to Christ. The same startling results were experienced as at Lancaster.

A revival campaign was next opened near Orrville, Ohio, for a period of four weeks. Here the same powerful messages, audience singing, and prayer support wrought mighty events. Dozens came forward in response to the invitation to seek a new or better experience with Jesus Christ. Here, too, there were the skeptical, the hangers-on, and those who wanted nothing of the meetings; but the interests of the masses prevailed.

Although no accurate count is known, it seems that approximately one-third of the people in the Ohio meetings were members of the Conservative Amish Mennonite Church, with a small sprinkling of Old Order Amish present. Many traveled twenty-five, fifty, and even one hundred miles. Members of the Wisler church, and various other conservative groups were also included. Many non-Mennonites also attended freely.

Following the successful Ohio meetings, the evangelistic team returned to Manheim, Pennsylvania, not far from the earlier location in Lancaster city. While the attendance at this place was fair, apparently opposition, mostly indirect, by some leaders of the church in that area had its effect: a lower number of people responded publicly.

During the winter of 1951-52, the Brunk brothers held two series of meetings in Florida, one in a Mennonite center, and the other in a non-Mennonite location. Calls to conduct revivals came from many states, and meetings were booked for a couple years in advance. Many requests were turned down.

The beginnings of this revival movement go back to 1946

when the two Brunk brothers, Lawrence and George, concluded revival meetings in Richmond, Virginia. On their way home from one of these services, the brothers agreed to enter evangelistic work together when possible.

When the plan did not seem to materialize, Lawrence one day stood in the midst of his poultry flock of five thousand broilers and asked the Lord to give him as many souls as there were chickens. He promised God that if he could make $5,000 clear, he would place the entire sum into the needed evangelistic equipment. By 1951, Lawrence was surprised bountifully by a $5,000 profit that grew to the astounding sum of $35,000. Lawrence placed this amount into expensive tents and traveling equipment. Soon the first revival campaign began in Lancaster.

Of the two brothers, George did the preaching. A Bible teacher at Eastern Mennonite College, he gave up his teaching to do full-time evangelistic work. He was a graduate of William and Mary College and of Union Theological Seminary, Richmond, Virginia. George was well aware of how church history has disclosed the excesses, weaknesses, and blessings of previous revival movements in various denominations. He also, by the nature of his training, was well acquainted with various aspects of theology. He handled well such persistent issues as divine healing, which arise at mass revival movements.

Both Lawrence and George are tall men, about six-feet-four, and have strong voices to accompany their stature. While they speak and preach frankly, one is impressed by their sincerity in wanting to make every meeting a Spirit-directed meeting. They have repeatedly opposed patterns of thinking that resemble hero worship and direct credit to the evangelists rather than to the Lord. They have insisted on this and asked no credit for themselves. As they wisely knew, the movement would crumble if God was forgotten.

Lawrence, the song leader, directed the large audiences in gospel songs and hymns. The audiences relished this part of the evening's program, as shown by the response.

What were the services like? There were daily prayer meetings, some preceding the evening meetings beginning at 7:30. Lawrence opened the meetings by having the audience sing many hymns and gospel songs. The a cappella, congregational-type singing seemed never to fail in lifting the spirits of those present.

After a short devotional period and further singing, George began his sermons. He spoke on such subjects as "God's Barriers to Hell," "From the Glory of Jericho to the Disgrace of Ai," and "The Sins of the Flesh and the Spirit." The sermons generally averaged an hour in length. After the sermon, the invitation was given. By this time the audience had heard much direct preaching, some that was new, and much that was familiar. The speaker drew his illustrations from life, from children, and practical experiences; all these had a tremendous effect in leading people to make decisions for Christ.

Most of us who were accustomed to sitting in our regular Mennonite services had a new experience when we witnessed those who walked forward in response to the invitation. For three nights, as I attended the meetings in my home community, I sat awed. One, two, three persons soon walked forward. The number increased so that I was unable to watch every part of the whole proceeding. I saw friends, relatives, and others walk to the front.

There were calls for additional counselors. The evening hour became late, 10:00 o'clock, and the meetings were still going strong, although some parents with children had wended their way out of the tent.

As counselors dealt with those seeking help, opportunity was given for those who wished to give their testimony for their Lord. There was no difficulty whatever in obtaining witnesses. As those in the prayer room found peace with God, they were urged to testify before the large audience.

As I entered into the joys and concerns of those who

spoke, I sat in my seat entranced, tears flowing down my cheeks at times. There was the seventy-year-old Christian who proclaimed his love for Christ. The very young, the youthful, the middle-aged, and the silver-haired gave their testimonies. To be sure, no golden-tongued oratory appeared. These were largely people who did not know what it meant to stand before others to witness. They walked timidly and stumbled in their speech. Many did not say all they wanted to say, forgetting some things under the stress.

Testimonies continued while those in the prayer room filed out to the platform. I was amazed to see an Amish man walk to the microphone. He stumbled a little in his speech, said something about finding his way, and then reached into his coat pocket and pulled out a pack of cigarettes. He handed them to George, who was standing nearby and guiding folks to the microphone. The cigarettes were plopped on the pulpit, and the joyful man completed his testimony. Another cigarette "sucker," as George put it, found his release. Soon another speaker was telling his story.

It was evident that many Christians had really found their Savior meaningful. A ten-minute period produced the following: A relative of mine, in halting English, told of the many children he had and how he wanted them to know Jesus Christ as Savior. Next two young girls sang their praises of God. Then came a young man who had been a Sunday school superintendent in a large church for several years. He said that he had malice in his heart and wanted to confess it. He had been influenced to make this confession, he explained, because his pastor had made a similar confession several days before; certainly he too should confess if his pastor could do it.

It was after eleven when the meetings were dismissed, though generally the huge tent was nearly empty. A few lingered, some with loved ones who had found Christ anew, and others with acquaintances, all marveling at this thing that had come to pass.

One evening I saw a young man whom I have known for twenty years suddenly walk to the front, where those seeking help were standing. In a moment, he went back to his seat—with a small, sleeping child on his shoulder. I soon understood what he had done. He had taken the child from the arms of his sister and her unfaithful husband so they could go into the prayer room unhindered. Soon the couple stood before the microphone, asking for prayers. The young husband, known to be unfaithful to his wife, pledged a new start.

On another evening, George gave the invitation, and the usual numbers walked to the front. Suddenly a man and a woman, who had walked down different aisles, raced across the front and hugged each other. Neither had known the other was present; they were husband and wife, separated for months.

For years in the Franconia Conference, a gang of young Mennonite men known as the Franconia Cowboys delighted in reckless driving and daring stunts, much to the chagrin of fellow church members. They were remarkably converted at the meetings and began engaging in prayer meetings and Christian work instead of the former rough stuff.

Obviously, the effect of the revivals in the local churches was profound. In the large Franconia Mennonite church, near Souderton, for example, in a regular Sunday morning service, over 130 responded to an invitation to confess sin and reconsecrate themselves to God. Significantly, this was the first invitation ever given in that church. In another church nearby, there were 85 confessions and testimonies on a Sunday morning during an outpouring of the Holy Spirit. Untold other miracles, including many acts of restitution not publicized, prevailed and continued over time.

The theme of the Brunk brothers revival campaigns was "The Whole Gospel for the Whole World." While the effects of the revivals can only be measured by God, visible results have been bountiful, and thousands have been blessed.

There were the obvious opponents, some skeptical and others feeling that mass revival techniques stir up individuals but do not give satisfactory answers. Yet the Brunks felt assured that they were being blessed of the Lord. Only time will reveal the great mysteries of the gospel; only time will disclose how many people have been saved through this revival movement.

This motto for George and Lawrence Brunk is fitting: "For we do not proclaim ourselves; we proclaim Christ Jesus as Lord and ourselves as your slaves for Jesus' sake" (2 Cor. 4:5).[54]

Mennonite Disaster Service on the job in the Kansas area.

INSET Torrential rains in the summer of 1951 produced many street scenes like this one in Topeka, Kansas.

Out of the Storm Clouds

Harley J. Stucky

*Mennonites are often known for their response to natur-
al disasters through Mennonite Disaster Service (MDS).
This network was born in Hesston, Kansas, when members of the Whitestone congregation asked how they
could continue the positive service to humanity they had
experienced in Civilian Public Service (CPS) during
World War II. That question found an answer in the
response to the Kansas floods of 1951.*

KANSANS WILL LONG remember 1951 as the year of the
floods. In that year Kansas suffered greater damage
from floods than droughts, tornadoes, and other disasters
had ever brought. Beginning the middle of May, heavy rains
continued through the middle of July, with periodic cycles of
flooding downpours.

By the time the third cycle of heavy rains struck Kansas
from June 21 to June 30, practically all of its major rivers in
the eastern third of the state were at record heights. The
flooding closed highways at some places, shut down
transcontinental train service, and caused damages mounting
in the millions of dollars.

In July, the rains continued with streams and rivers rising
again to disastrous levels in the state. The cities of Marion
and Florence were flooded four times in less than two
months. Other cities completely or partly inundated were

Manhattan, Topeka, Ottawa, Osawatomie, Independence, Emporia, Abilene, Salina, Clay Center, and Halstead. Scores of other towns suffered heavy losses from the raging water.

Many of the Kansas streams converge in the northeast area of the state and empty into the Kansas or Kaw River. The two major cities along this river, Topeka and Kansas City, bore the full brunt of flood waters that reached all-time record height.

As the floodwaters rushed downstream, weary people began the pitiful task of reclaiming their homes, farms, and industries, and of reestablishing themselves. In Kansas and Missouri, forty-nine persons died, more than one hundred thousand (some say 167,000) were left homeless, and two million acres of rich farmland were inundated; total property losses exceeded one billion dollars. All this was the result of the Kansas floods. Kansas marks 1951 as the year of the Great Floods, or of many floods, or of two months of floods.

Nevertheless, every cloud has its silver lining; certainly this was true in 1951. None of the flood refugees suffered from lack of food, shelter, or medical care. In most places, emergency facilities were adequate. Thousands of volunteer workers and nameless heroes came to the rescue of their less fortunate brothers and sisters.

As the floodwaters rose and fell in May, June, and July of 1951, thousands of neighbors and friends extended helping hands to provide aid, regardless of class, color, political creed, or religious faith. Everywhere volunteers maintained dikes by sandbagging and patrolling, helped to evacuate those in the path of the surging waters, or rescued marooned people.

The Red Cross spent more than twelve million dollars for emergency aid, rehabilitation, and to replace household furniture and farm supplies.

Among those who sought to alleviate the suffering and misery of this disaster were the various Mennonite groups, such as the Amish, Mennonite Brethren, Krimmer Mennonite

Brethren, (Old) Mennonites, General Conference Mennonites, and the Church of God in Christ, Mennonite (Holdeman). The burning convictions of peace and nonresistance, and the practical application of love, coupled with years of toil on their farms, had prepared them for an occasion such as this.

During the emergency, Mennonites helped in the rescue work, gave food and clothing, and helped to provide shelter. After the floodwaters receded, hundreds helped in the cleanup phase of the operation. Finally, when most other groups had forgotten their stricken neighbors, Mennonites were still helping in the rehabilitation of flood victims who could not help themselves.

When the first flash floods inundated various central Kansas towns in May 1951, volunteers helped in the cleanup and in patrolling the dikes. Men from the (Old) Mennonite congregations of Hesston and from the Bethel College Mennonite Church at North Newton helped to patrol the banks of the Arkansas River. Day and night they watched for possible "water boils" in the dikes and behind the dikes.

When the torrential rains of July 10 and succeeding days swept the state, Mennonites were involved with rescuing those marooned and helped to provide emergency rations and supplies, particularly to those in central Kansas, as at Marion and Florence. The Bethel College Peace and Emergency Relief Committee sent sandwiches and other supplies to Marion and Florence.

At Florence the canteen, under the general direction of the Red Cross, was open for twenty-four hours a day and served some six to nine hundred persons. Merchants of Newton and surrounding towns, churches, and other organized groups—all did what they could to alleviate suffering. The Eden Mennonite Church at Moundridge sent two truckloads of food and clothing to Florence in less than forty-eight hours.

Many of the flood refugees had fled their homes in the night, saving nothing except the clothes they were wearing.

All the furniture, family keepsakes, family albums and photographs, and other valuables were ruined. Many residents were in a state of shock; nearly every person could tell a tale of heroism and tragedy. It was the duty of the helpers to listen sympathetically to these stricken people and to counsel them with words of wisdom.

While the floodwaters remained, the residents of inundated homes spent hours standing at the water's edge, waiting for it to recede so they could return to their homesteads, repair the damage, and start life anew. With the subsiding waters, the second phase of operations commenced. The cleanup phase began at Halstead and other places on July 13. On Saturday, July 14, the waters receded far enough so that men could begin cleanup operations in Marion and, to a limited extent, in Florence.

Volunteers came from Moundridge, Inman, Buhler, Goessel, Hillsboro, Newton, and other places. They were armed with trucks, shovels, mops, rubber hoses, brooms, scoops, and other tools.

They went down this street and up that street, from one house to another. They helped to carry out debris, tables, chairs, other furniture, appliances, papers, bedding, and mattresses waterlogged and so heavy that it was a good job for four men to carry them out. After the rubbish was carried out, the men would begin to scoop out the silt; it often was from two to twelve inches deep. The last step in the process was to sweep and wash out the house.

On Sunday, July 15, the same process continued in many other towns, among them Florence. The ox had fallen in the ditch, to use biblical phraseology, and Mennonites did what they could, even on Sunday. In Florence members of many groups helped the local citizens to salvage what they could and remove the rest. There were some fifty to seventy-five people from the Hoffnungsau congregation alone; they participated as vigorously as any in the cleanup of Florence on this particular Sunday afternoon.

As the floodwaters receded in other towns, volunteers again moved in, helping in the cleanup operations in Topeka and even in Kansas City. Most of these volunteers came from central Kansas, but some also came from Nebraska, Oklahoma, Missouri, and other places.

Some months after the cleanup operation, when all the publicity had died down, Mennonites made arrangements with the Red Cross to rehabilitate some of the homes. They chose buildings where private resources, insurance money, and other aid did not enable owners to hire enough workers to restore their homes. In a few cases these volunteers helped to stretch the money received from the Red Cross, particularly for the poor residents in north Topeka.

With the supervision of a continuing foreman, carloads of men kept coming into Topeka from central Kansas to repair homes and churches in a needy section of north Topeka. The Mennonite Central Committee (MCC) sent a continuing team of reconstruction workers from Voluntary Service. They, together with other volunteer workers who came in, built homes that still stand as a testimony.

In Topeka, there was a continuing Mennonite witness: vacation Bible school teachers, a Voluntary Service unit, and a I-W alternative service unit. Various types of fellowship continued between people of color in north Topeka and some white Mennonites of central Kansas. Many of these ministers had longtime standing invitations to preach to the black churches of this area.

The first phase of disaster work is the most glamorous and the most newsworthy; hence, many people respond. But as the publicity dies down, the response to the cleanup phase and rehabilitation work begins to waver, and finally it dies out. In the first phase, people are motivated by sympathy and sheer curiosity, but in the second and third phases, their motivation needs a deeper rootage. They need motivation emerging from a faith written into the very fabric of their thoughts and lives.

Such helpers must also be in vocations from which they can readily be released for periods of time. Most Mennonites were prepared for this work by being farmers, accustomed to hard work, and by holding the conviction that service to others is an essential part of the Christian faith.

Mennonites received many expressions of appreciation and thanks for their service. The Marion Chamber of Commerce expressed thanks in the *Marion Record Review* of July 19, 1951, to "Hillsboro, Lehigh, Goessel, Pilsen, Durham, Tampa, Canton, Peabody, Newton, Lincolnville, Lost Springs, Ramona, Hesston, McPherson, Galva, Moundridge, Canada, Aulne, and other towns, communities, churches, and individuals."

Similar statements of appreciation appeared in other newspapers. Perhaps the most significant are the following. First a quotation from a letter written to the *Evening-Kansan* and appearing in its editorial of July 23, 1951:

> We wish to thank all those who helped in any way in our recent flood disaster in Marion and especially the Bethel College students who worked so faithfully helping clean up in the courthouse and elsewhere.
>
> It seems to us that these students are learning things about life that are not found in textbooks.
> —*Board of County Commissioners, Marion County*

Another illustration of appreciation comes from the *Florence Bulletin,* of August 2, 1951. The story, entitled "The Mennonites Helped Florence Recuperate from Flood Waters," was written by Gordon P. Martin, a member of the *Topeka Journal* staff.

> As the years go on and some of the memories of the Great Flood of 1951 begin to fade, there is one thing residents will not allow new generations to forget. That is the way the hardworking, God-fearing Mennonite

farmers have come from miles away to give Florence a
helping hand. They scrubbed this town of 1,000 on
their hands and knees. They have helped many a flood-
stricken resident and businessman to get back on his
feet, cleaning both homes and stores. They have found
no chore too hard, no task too difficult. . . . They came
from Moundridge, Goessel, Inman, Yoder, Hillsboro,
Burns, Newton, Elbing, Galva, Durham, Buhler,
Hesston, Hutchinson, and Canton, armed with mops,
buckets, muscles, and their well-known enmity for dirt
and untidiness.

There are various sects in their ranks, but all were
friends of Florence, as they were of nearby bigger
Marion. . . . The Mennonites . . . will know the grate-
fulness of Florence for years to come.

As a result of the floods of 1951, an inter-Mennonite
organization was created and later came to be known as the
Mennonite Disaster Service (MDS). The witness of MDS—
the silver lining that resulted from the storm clouds of the
1951 Kansas floods—lives on fifty years later.[55]

Cooking for better health: MCC provides lessons on food preparation, Kimpese, Congo.

INSET Orie O. Miller, the "Thomas Edison" of church ministries, and co-author, Peter J. Dyck.

French Fries and World Missions

Peter J. Dyck and John M. Bender

Orie O. Miller (1892-1977) felt called to the ministry. Three times the lot passed over him; yet he became one of the most remarkable, innovative, and courageous Mennonite leaders of his generation. He keenly sensed the interrelatedness of the score or more agencies, Mennonite and nondenominational, on whose boards of directors he sat; he saw all of these agencies were part of the church and its mission. His vision and utter self-discipline made all this possible.[56]

O RIE MILLER WAS a Mennonite (MC) layman, an administrator who bridged the worlds of business and church. The eldest in the family of Bishop D. D. and Jeanette Hostetler Miller, Middlebury, Indiana, Orie directed the farmwork when his father traveled as an evangelist. He wanted to serve the church full-time as a schoolteacher, minister, or missionary. Before college he taught public school. After his freshman year at Goshen College, he directed Goshen's school of business.

Orie graduated from Goshen College in 1915. That August he married classmate Elta Wolf. The couple moved to Akron, Pennsylvania, where Orie soon became a part owner of the shoe company headed by his father-in-law. Despite the growing success of the shoe business, Orie still felt called to church work, particularly the ministry. Three times he was a ministerial candidate at Ephrata Mennonite Church, but the lot did not fall on him. He said of his first experience in the lot, "I just couldn't understand it. God didn't confirm my call. These were the most difficult days of my life."

Annually Orie read the Bible through from cover to cover; hence, he could quote Scripture as others quoted newspapers. Eventually, the church did call Orie to help in relief work in Syria and Armenia after World War I. As church leaders met in Lancaster, Pennsylvania, to discuss a request for Mennonite workers for overseas relief, "Father leaned over to me and said, 'Orie, shouldn't you volunteer for this?'" With his wife's assent and a leave from the business for several months, Orie sailed for Beirut on the *USS Pensacola* on January 25, 1919.

Three months after his return, at a meeting regarding Mennonite needs in Russia, Orie again said yes when asked to go. But how could he represent all the committees? The idea for a Mennonite Central Committee (MCC) was born and became a reality on July 21, 1920. Orie was chosen to direct the first unit of volunteers. However, Orie's father-in-law, heading a business adversely affected by the postwar economic slump, was not ready to release him again. "You can't mix business and the church," he said. "You must give full time to the business or leave it." Orie went to Russia.

Orie and Clayton Kratz got into Russia and made arrangements to do relief work. However, the overthrow of the Wrangel government prevented plans from being carried out. Orie returned to Constantinople and organized relief activities among Russian refugees pouring into that city. He returned to Akron in spring 1921. He and his father-in-law eventually arrived at an arrangement whereby Orie gave about two-thirds time to the business and one-third to the church. Church work centered in world relief, missions, and education. He was executive secretary of MCC, 1935-58.

In 1940, at age forty-eight, Orie was ready to devote even more time to the church. He turned over the sales work to others he had trained and continued as director and secretary-treasurer of Miller Hess and Company; president of Highland Shoe Company, also in Akron; and treasurer of A. N. Wolf Shoe Company, Denver, Pennsylvania.

Orie influenced the church in the vast program of Mennonite relief and refugee resettlement, the Civilian Public Service (CPS) Program, the organization and growth of Mennonite Economic Development Associates (MEDA), the organization of Menno Travel Service (MTS) and Mennonite Mutual Aid (MMA), and in many other Mennonite and interchurch causes.

Orie spelled out his philosophy of administration in three words: *freedom, responsibility*, and *structure*.

> The administrator's job is to build a structure so everyone knows what his job is and to whom he is responsible. The capable administrator helps people work together without wasting time, fighting, or stepping on each other's toes. He helps people become a team. When a person accurately senses the structure and fulfills his responsibility, he is free.

Orie and Elta had five children. Elta died in 1958. In 1960 Orie married Elta Sensenig. Orie died at the Landis Retirement Home near Lancaster in January 1977.

Orie Miller was not without a sense of humor. He claimed that he could travel around the world, which he did about seventeen times, and order his meals anywhere with three words: *omelette, cocoa* (or *chocolate*), and *french fries*. When he did just that in Paris, the annoyed French waiter snapped back, "We don't fry the French," and refused to take the order. Orie's philosophic response was characteristic: "That's how you get when you lose an empire." France had just "lost" Morocco and Algeria.

Someone said that Orie Miller saw more of the world than Marco Polo, opened more mission fields than David Livingstone, and was as innovative in church ministries as Thomas Edison was in technology. He was God's gift to the church.[57]

The Emancipation Proclamation, January 1, 1863, illustrated by Thomas Nast.

INSET Martin Luther King Jr. and Guy F. Hershberger at Goshen College, 1963.

Come Sunday, Will We Be a True Communion?

James Samuel Logan

*Robert, Mary Elizabeth, and Cloyd Carter are the first
known African Americans in the Mennonite Church. On
April 21, 1897, they became members of Lauver
Mennonite Church, a Lancaster Conference congregation
in Pennsylvania.*[58] *James and Rowena Lark were well
known for organizing summer Bible schools, and as energetic and visionary church planters. James H. Lark
became the first ordained African American Mennonite
minister on October 6, 1946. He served Bethel Mennonite
Church in Chicago, where he was ordained to the office of
bishop, September 26, 1954. One hundred years after the
Carters became Mennonites, Dwight McFadden was
installed as moderator of the Mennonite Church (1997).*

*The one hundred years—from the first membership to
the first moderator—are marked by successes and failures, joy and pain, hope and disillusionment. African
American and European American Mennonites have
been on a journey, learning how to be a true expression
of the body of Christ. James Samuel Logan, now a Ph.D.
candidate in Religion and Society at Princeton
Theological Seminary, tells of his journey as an African
American Mennonite.*

I WAS BORN THE second child of an unmarried teenage mother who, by the time she was twenty-seven, had conceived seven children by three different men. There was much misery for my mother and her children, and there was much love, compassion, and commitment, as well. My mother, to this very day, continues to teach me much about life. I respect her and love her dearly.

I believe that my mother and the births of her children will shatter many myths and images. While my mother did not conceive her children in the mythologically perfect two-parent, 2.5 children, all-American "Dream Team" family, she is as committed as any parent to nurturing and guiding her children along the path of self-dignity and self-worth.

One of the key lessons I learned from my mother can be summed up in the words of the existentialist writer-philosopher Albert Camus:

> Poverty was not a calamity for me.
>   It was always balanced by the
>   richness of light . . .
>   circumstances helped me.
> To correct a natural indifference I was
>   placed halfway
>   between
>   misery and the sun.
> Misery kept me from believing that all was
>   well under the sun, and
>   the sun taught me that history wasn't everything.[59]

My four sisters, two brothers, and I grew up with my mother in Harlem and the South Bronx in New York City. From about the ages of eight to seventeen, I attended Camp Deerpark, owned and operated by the New York City Mennonite churches. This and other church-related experiences acquainted me with various peace church agencies.

In general, I have been influenced, burdened, helped, and

hindered by people who are rooted deeply within the Anabaptist religious tradition. Much of this interaction took place in and around Glad Tidings Mennonite Church in the Bronx and at Seventh Avenue Mennonite Church in Harlem.

Inside the Anabaptist tradition, I was affected by the words and the writings of educators Hubert Brown and Zenebe Abebe, Spanish historian Rafael Falcón, theologian José Ortiz, Old Testament scholar Wilma Bailey, biologist and bishop Monroe Yoder, New Testament scholar Gertrude Roten, and historian C. J. Dyck. These elders of our faith tradition and others helped me see clearly that the story of the African American experience in North America is also a part of the peace church experience.

The Peace Church's Ambivalence

Black Africans first arrived in the American colonies in 1619. They came from the West Indies on a Dutch ship named *Jesus* and landed at Jamestown, Virginia. In 1688, sixty-nine years after the landing of *Jesus*, the peace church, or some portion of it, first went on record as being opposed to slavery.

It is clear to me that some portions of the peace church have historically become increasingly conscious and concerned about racism. Yet I contend that our beloved Anabaptist community has more often than not quietly acquiesced to the racism of the surrounding culture and, therefore, participated in it.

From the start, the peace church legacy on racism in the United States has been ambivalent. For example, in 1924 a group of congregations now known as the Allegheny Mennonite Conference courageously passed a strong resolution against the Ku Klux Klan because of the group's discrimination against "Jews, Catholics, and [African Americans]." In that same year, however, another district conference encouraged establishing separate congregations for African Americans and cautioned against "close social relations" or intermarriage. It is this latter view, in various manifestations, that guides the core masses in today's peace churches, at least as I interpret its history.

I am continually and critically affected by a whole historical legacy of racism and a multitude of influences other than those of the Anabaptist peace churches. Because of these other forces, the peace church must seek to create a much closer approximation of the kingdom of God on earth.

For example, we who call ourselves the peace church in the United States must continue (and in too many cases begin) to examine the African American historical resistance to the American nightmare and the African American contribution to the so-called American Dream. The peace church must engage itself in serious dialogue with resistance traditions, just like the ones embodied vicariously in the lives and deaths of Sojourner Truth, Harriet Tubman, Malcolm X, Martin Luther King Jr., and Fannie Lou Hamer. Malcolm X and King, along with many other men and women, represent a blood sacrifice for the salvation of a nation that still, in great measure, refuses to be redeemed.

Our Collusion with Racism

Indeed, if we are to find the truth so often buried beneath the untruth, we must create new models of community. We must cultivate the kinds of children, men, and women who can live new models of servanthood and love in the name of Christ.

I am speaking of the kinds of models that question our peace church's silent assumption about race—as well as class and gender. I am talking about the kind of church community that will foster a Christlike integrity challenging us to question our greatest icons and our most revered traditions. It also is my hope that we would emphasize the importance of caring and compassionate critique.

It will be crucial for the peace church to acknowledge its historical collusion in the sin of racism, and then to do something redemptive and sacrificial, reconciling and prophetic. The peace church has accomplished much that it can be proud of when it comes to dealing forthrightly with the racism of its church institutions. Yet the peace church must also confess that it has too often hindered where it might have helped, and been evasive when it was morally bound to be forthright. In many instances, church institutions continue to separate peace church believers on the basis of race, even though the church declares its mission as one that seeks to demonstrate God's love to all.

Many people want to believe we can respond to the human condition of brokenness in the peace church but stay entirely divorced from the historical reality of racism as a serious and ongoing human tragedy. I am disheartened to see, in stark detail, how soon and how utterly often we forget or ignore our church's and nation's history.

We forget why Martin Luther King Jr. wrote *Why We Can't Wait* in 1964. We forget about the life and times of Fannie Lou Hammer in the middle part of this century. We forget why Langston Hughes wrote about *The Ways of White Folks* in 1934. We forget about preachers like Amanda Berry Smith and justice advocates like Sojourner Truth. We forget the struggles of James Lark, the first African American bishop in the Mennonite Church.

We forget about the suffering of the early Anabaptist believers in Switzerland, South Germany, Russia, and elsewhere. I see people like Conrad Grebel and Felix Manz, as well as other women and men in the early Anabaptist tradition, as struggling till death for a believers church faith perspective. At its best, these Anabaptist martyrs stand neck and neck with the struggle of those named and unnamed radiantly dark African faces that swung grotesquely from the trees of the American democratic contradiction. I speak of those same faces and burning flesh that Billie Holliday sang so eloquently about in her melancholy anthem "Strange Fruit."

In general, those representing dominant power within today's Anabaptist peace church too often forget about the loving, suffering, and triumphant Christ of history. As a collective group, today's peace church tends to forget (or pretends to forget) that a move to include the gifts of *all* peace church members, regardless of their race or ethnicity, is not a struggle that is happening for the first time in our church's history. Our current struggles do not exist in some kind of metaphysical vacuum, detached from the ways we live our lives in our church structures and communities.

Beyond Good Intentions

Let me speak more plainly, with nothing but love and a deep sense of sorrow. Many European American Anabaptists generally seem not to care about making serious and lasting mutually empowering and vulnerable connections with the diverse cultures, traditions, and histories of our current church structure in North America. Furthermore, *beyond merely good intentions*, they do not seem to care about having critical masses of other than white folks as friends, acquaintances, and colleagues in their daily lives.

We, the peace church, must learn to respond to our own devastating legacy of noninclusiveness with the same vigor of attitude and deliberate spiritual fortitude that we used to face Hurricane Andrew, the Midwest floods, and the misery of Rwanda.

If we as a people can begin (or continue) to enter multiracial and multiethnic communities, we might be better prepared to understand words like these from Charles Lawrence in the *Stanford Law Review*:

> Racism in America is much more complex than either the conscious conspiracy of a power elite or the simple delusion of a few ignorant bigots. It is part of our common historical experience and, therefore, a part of our culture. [Racism continues to arise] from the assump-

tions we have learned to make about the world, ourselves, and others, as well as from the patterns of our [most] fundamental social activities.

Like when we go to church on Sunday morning.

Let Us Learn . . .

It is tragic that for African Americans, the historical public meaning of Christianity in the United States justified, among other atrocities, bringing our foreparents as human cargo from the shores of Mother Africa on ships with strange-sounding names, such as *Gift of God*, *Integrity*, and *John the Baptist*.

This brand of Christianity cannot be tolerated in the peace church today. As historian Vincent Harding once said, "Let us learn to listen and act upon some of the points of view of women and men who have heard vaguely that we, [the peace church], have a witness concerning peace and reconciliation." Then we might truly represent the poor in spirit, the ones who mourn, the meek, the ones who hunger and thirst after righteousness, the merciful, the pure in heart, the peacemakers, and the one(s) persecuted for righteousness' sake (Matt. 5:1-10).

There is a pervasive spiritual impoverishment that grows daily in America. Increasingly we are witnessing the collapse of spiritual communities—the kinds of communities that help people love themselves and others; the kinds of communities that help families and neighborhoods face despair, disease, and life and death with love, dignity, commitment, and decency.

If, in the name of Christ, we wish to be a meaningful presence in the face of our increasing national nihilism and xenophobia, we must, with fear and trembling, as historian Vincent Harding tried to tell the peace church in 1967, be willing to be driven beyond all limits of physical and intellectual and spiritual safety that we know now; then the anointing may come. Then the broken victims will leap for joy at our appearance, and the humiliated will sing a song of praise. (at the Eighth Mennonite World Conference, Amsterdam, The Netherlands)

Let us learn to live in community with those we consider to be the so-called others. Let us learn to make an understanding of diverse histories, cultures, and experiences crucial to our faith perspective and to our very development at human beings. Let us interact with one another as wine, old and mature, and as bread, freshly baked. Then, come Sunday, we might represent a true communion.[60]

A healing touch under the banner "House of Medicine, In the Name of Christ."

INSET U.S. troops landing near the Cambodian border during Operation Ripping Mustang, January 1966.

A Wanderer Comes Home

Beryl Forrester

*Mennonites are known as one of the historic peace
churches, along with the Church of the Brethren, and the
Quakers. Menno Simons wrote, "The regenerated do not
go to war nor engage in strife." Menno echoed the call
of Jesus to be finished with war, to lay down the sword,
and instead, to take up the cross and the towel, symbols
of sacrificial love. In times of war, Mennonites have
struggled to find ways to be faithful to this call, amid the
militaristic patriotism of their neighbors. During the
Vietnam War, Mennonites were ambivalent, reflecting the
turmoil of the country. While some identified with the
popular anti-war movement, many more were uncom-
fortable with such overt resistance. Some Mennonite
young men resisted the draft, most registered as conscientious objectors, and a few joined the military.*

*Cy Smith was a typical American kid in the 1960s, who
enlisted in the United States Army. His pilgrimage took
him from the battlefields of Cambodia to the campus of
Western Mennonite School. This is the story of Smith's
spiritual homecoming.*

IN 1994, THE Salem (Ore.) Mennonite Church was preparing to commission two of its members, Ken and Mabel Snyder, for work in Laos with Mennonite Central Committee. Meanwhile, a landslide of partially healed memories was being unleashed for another member, Cy Smith. In the days before their leaving, the Snyders talked about their upcoming responsibilities, including the bombie project, an attempt to clear the Laotian countryside of unexploded bombs dropped by the United States military.

Cy Smith had played a part in putting those bombs there. Now, thirty years later, he belonged to a community of people working to heal the wounds of war and hatred. As he stood arm-in-arm with Ken and Mabel at their commissioning service, he said, "I am grateful to God that I can be part of a people who are helping to clean up the mayhem I helped create."

How did all this come to be? In 1965, at age twenty, Cy faced some difficulties and turned to the army as a solution to his problems. At 6:00 a.m. on May 25 of that year, Cy scrambled to attention for the first time with twenty other enlistees at the Fort Bragg (N.C.) boot camp. The recruits were ordered to arrange themselves shoulder-to-shoulder according to height, the tallest man to the right.

Years later, Cy reflected on those experiences in boot camp: "Those weeks were a well-programmed regimen to cast youthful enthusiasm and aspirations into cogs for the military machine." Youth's innocence and awkwardness needed to be hardened into a warrior's violence and willingness to die on a battlefield. "Can you imagine what it would be like to die in a burning tank?" Cy wondered aloud, his eyes squinting. "Boot camp taught us that to survive we must give unquestioning obedience to our commanding officer and absolutely conform to the goals of the platoon."

A boot camper, Cy recalled, who failed to keep up with the group, was given a "blanket party." His buddies would throw a blanket over him and then have a free-for-all of kicking and stomping on him. The drill sergeant simply reported that the trainee had fallen down a flight of stairs during an exercise.

After boot camp, Cy became part of the Special Forces, known to the public as Green Berets. He received special training as a radioman so he could penetrate enemy lines and communicate with bomber pilots, helping them pinpoint ground targets. His special campaign's classified mission was to disrupt the Ho Chi Minh Trail, the major supply line from China to Southeast Asia. That particular mission, known as "MacNamara's electric fence," was scrubbed when U.S. Senator Fulbright persuaded President Lyndon Johnson that such an action would inevitably bring China directly into the war. So Cy found himself involved in a variety of other jungle operations.

On patrols as ground soldiers, Cy and a few others were parachuted into remote areas of the Cambodian jungle. They would crawl around in the swampy mire, looking for supply depots, rest areas, and hospitals operated by the enemy. After they radioed locations of such installations to the nearest U.S. airbase, bombers would then "carpet bomb" a thousand-square-meter grid, completely annihilating the targeted installation. "Under pressure from those thousand-pound bombs, the jungle literally fell apart," Cy reported.

In a combat setting, Cy said, "one also experiences a kind of personal devastation. There are wounds to the soul from which one can never fully recover. Yes, I know God's love and forgiveness, but the scars are still there."

Reviewing how his thinking about the military evolved, Cy noted, "In my adolescence the military appeared to be a very attractive option. It seemed to be a way to climb, to get an education, and to survive. Also, the messages from my family, church, and community made military service the noble and honorable thing to do." By the end of his three years in the military, however, all those myths lay abandoned, like so much war material on a deserted battlefield.

"Slowly, I began to realize that I was part of a powerful, ugly war machine, a machine that turns people into robots of destruction," Cy admits today. "To succeed, one must acquire an utter disregard for the value of the individual."

During his early training at Ft. Bragg, Cy watched as his personhood was slowly and almost imperceptibly obliterated; all value was focused on the survival of the company. The recruits were taught that the enemy was a wild animal to be annihilated for the good of society.

Once on the frontlines, Cy witnessed that training being translated into devastating reality. Even the Southeast Asian allies he was sent to train were considered subhuman and backward by the U.S. military.

As Cy became increasingly disgusted with the ugliness of the war and the military, he was finding new friends among the people of Thailand. His gregarious nature was met with legendary Thai hospitality and resulted in mutual appreciation. The Thai people welcomed him into their homes, where he learned something of the richness of their ancient culture. He was particularly impressed by the Thai people's deep commitment to family.

Since he had already experienced a sense of wrongness in his involvement in Vietnam, Cy began to solidify his pacifist thinking in college after finishing his military service. He became caught up in the anti-Vietnam War fervor, becoming involved in antidraft counseling and organizing war protests. "In my youthful enthusiasm, I was out to help reform our society," Cy said. "I wanted to help create a society where everyone's rights are respected, pacifism is the norm, and the environment is revered.

As reality set in, it became apparent to Cy that society would not be reformed by student protesters. His world began to spiral inward. As an ex-student, Cy drifted all over North and South America, searching for that ever-elusive utopia.

Some twenty years later, in the late 1980s, "the wanderer

began to come home," Cy said. He met Sandy Haury, a woman from Mennonite background. They married and became part of Salem Mennonite Church, where, Cy reported, "We found a community of evangelical Christians serious about peace and justice in our world."

Cy began to work for peace. In 1994 he became part of a task group in Salem that attempted, though unsuccessfully, to prevent Reserve Officers' Training Corp (ROTC) from coming into the Salem-Keiser public schools.

Later Cy joined the staff of the Western Mennonite High School as head of maintenance. "Now I live and work in a setting where pacifism and peacemaking are the norm," Cy rejoiced. "In Christian community several things are happening to me. I continue to experience healing for the wounds in my soul as a Vietnam veteran. I find nurture and hope as I live and work with other Christian, and I am able to be an active peacemaker."

In his position at the school, Cy has been able to put into practice his ideals for stewardship of the environment. His responsibilities on campus also have put him in constant contact with young people who are trying to sort through their understanding of God's peace and justice. Cy has been able to share with them his journey as a peacemaker and as a "wanderer who has come home."[61]

A congregation at worship: where the Word is preached, Goshen College chapel service in the 1960s.

INSET Marilyn Miller and Emma Richards took the first high steps into pastoral ministry.

The Threshold Is High

Anne Stuckey

*On January 15, 1911, Ann Jemima Allebach became the
first woman on record to be ordained a minister by
Mennonites in North America. N. B. Grubb officiated in
that service at First Mennonite Church, Philadelphia.
Born May 8, 1874, Ann was baptized at Eden
Mennonite Church, Schwenksville, Pennsylvania. In
1893 she attended classes at New York University,
Columbia University, and Union Theological Seminary
in New York City. There she took part in the women's
suffrage movement and served among the poor.
Wondering if she should be ordained, she spoke to her
mentor, N. B. Grubb, and her own pastor, J. W. Schantz,
and they agreed. She drew large audiences when she
occasionally returned to Mennonite churches as a guest
preacher. In 1916 she began serving a Reformed congregation, then died of a heart attack in 1918.[62]*

*In the following account, Emma Richards and Marilyn
Miller reflect on their years of ministry at a celebration
held at Associated Mennonite Biblical Seminary, Elkhart,
Indiana, on January 26, 1998. The writer, Anne Stuckey,
is a pastor who has served nine years as Minister of
Congregational Leadership at Mennonite Board of
Congregational Ministries, Elkhart, Indiana.*

A JAPANESE EXPRESSION, "The threshold is high," describes the first high step into a traditional Japanese home. At the entrance you must first remove your shoes and then take a high step over the threshold to enter.

This image also fits the experience of the first women called to congregational pastoral ministry twenty-five years ago. Emma Richards was called to such a ministry by Lombard (Ill.) Mennonite Church and was ordained by the Illinois Conference in 1973, making her the first ordained woman in the Mennonite Church. In 1976, Marilyn Miller was ordained by the Western District Conference of the General Conference Mennonite Church to serve as co-pastor of Arvada (Colo.) Mennonite Church.

Emma made some early decisions that provided the framework for her years as a pastor. In her spiritual life, she decided not to let her inner well run dry. Even though this meant getting up at four in the morning to pray, read Scripture and meditate, this daily connection with God made ministry possible.

In the congregation, she decided that the agenda for ministry would come from the congregation, not from her, and that she would lead by loving the congregation, its purpose, and its mission. Emma preached well-prepared, expository sermons, keeping Jesus central both in sermons and in prayers. She paired this priority with being an Anabaptist-Mennonite pastor in teaching and in living.

At a time when women pastors were scarce and often called upon to serve the broader church, Emma decided to stay in the congregation, especially in the early years, rather than going out to preach in other churches or to lead conferences on women in ministry. She wanted to allay fears that with a woman as pastor, men would not come to church, attendance would decline, and men would not go to a woman pastor for help. But this was not the experience of Lombard Mennonite Church.

What sustained this call for Emma was the certainty that

she was always inside the will of God for her life. She knew that Jesus was near her and that the Holy Spirit was guiding her.

When you hear Emma talk today, you notice her thankfulness. She is thankful for the overarching mercy of God through Jesus Christ, for early church leaders who trusted her when others were raising their eyebrows. She is thankful for a new generation of women who have heard the call and taken the step into pastoral leadership with integrity and skill. She is also thankful for her children; her husband, Joe; and the home and the congregation in which she grew up.

Marilyn Miller tells of hearing the call for more pastors when she was in elementary school in the late 1940s: "The church at large is greatly in need of pastors. Pray that more young men will open their ears and hear the call of the Lord." Standing in her backyard in Kansas and looking up at the stars, she asked God, "If you are in need of more pastors, why wasn't I created a man?"

After watching her father, who was a pastor, she knew that she, too, would love to be a pastor. But it wasn't until after marriage and after saying at home to raise her children for nine years that Marilyn even had the chance to prepare for ministry. God made that possible.

Marilyn's father, Milo Kauffman, supported her call to ministry and never questioned her ordination. After being president of Hesston (Kan.) College for nineteen years, he had opportunities to travel extensively throughout the church. When people asked what he thought about women being called to ministry, he would say, "When I look at women around the church using their gifts, I have to say with Peter, "If then God gave them the same gift that he gave us, . . . who [am] I that I could hinder God?" (Acts 11:17).

When Marilyn was questioning whether it was necessary to be ordained in order to pastor, a saint from the Arvada congregation climbed the hill behind the church with her just to talk. The woman said, "Maybe if you allow us to celebrate the gifts God has given you, then we can celebrate the gifts God has given us a little better."

God, children, congregation, and family all came together in Marilyn's pastoral ministry. Her reflections on the death of her son in a kayaking accident, her daughter's wedding, and the similarities between church planting in Boulder (Col.) and developing a home—these all bring one back to the totality of life in ministry; it includes all these things. "Relationships in life are most important," she said, "love for God and love for people."

Emma said it and Marilyn echoed that the threshold to ministry is indeed high. But they are glad they took the high step. In doing so, they are thankful they were upheld by God's grace and mercy through Jesus Christ. If there is any glory, they said, it belongs to God. Menno Simons wrote of the vocation of preachers: "They were driven into this office by the Spirit of God, with pious hearts."[63] That is true of both Marilyn Miller and Emma Richards.

Women called to ministry have experienced many disappointments and hurts in the past twenty-five years. Nevertheless, God's grace gave each the power to take that high step into ministry.[64]

Communion Balinese style at the Asia Mennonite Conference, Dhyana Pura, Indonesia, 1998.

INSET Mesach Krisetya, the Fireproof Man and president of Mennonite World Conference.

A Fireproof Man
Loyal to Christ

Phyllis Pellman Good

*We are entering the twenty-first century with a new
awareness: African, Asian, and Latin American
Mennonites outnumber European and North American
Mennonites. These "daughter churches" express a passion for mission and service that also exceeds that of the
"mother churches." Mennonite World Conference president Mesach Krisetya has demonstrated that passion.
Under his leadership, we will likely see an increased role
for MWC, a role with greater influence on the "mother
churches" in Europe and North America.*

———

MENNONITE WORLD CONFERENCE'S president is a tall,
long-fingered Indonesian of Chinese ancestry who
picked his own name. Chinese-Indonesians are a racial
minority in Mesach Krisetya's country. His chosen faith
placed him within yet another minority group; Christians are
about 12 percent of the population in Indonesia, and
Muslims are 87-90 percent.

The meaning of Mesach's name reflects his clear-eyed
understanding and his commitments: "fireproof man loyal to
Christ." The name may be more fitting than Mesach realized
when he chose it. Today there are growing threats against
Indonesian Christians' lives; here and there women have

been raped and churches burned. Christians are perceived to be disloyal to the government and the majority religion.

Raised in a family that practiced Confucianism and ancestor worship, Mesach was growing up as World War II rumbled through the Pacific and as his own country tried to foist off Dutch rule. "Schools kept changing during those years from being run by the Dutch, to being run by the Japanese, to being run finally by the Indonesians. My high schooling got delayed; I didn't graduate until I was twenty-one." He persisted because of his own interest, but also because his parents planned that he would go to medical school to become a doctor.

Mesach didn't object to the goal, but he couldn't shake a pair of questions: Who am I? What will my future be? "I was never satisfied, even when people said I was doing well," Mesach recalls.

In the middle of all this uncertainty, "a good friend invited me to attend a Bible camp with him. I had no idea what the Bible was, but he was a friend, so I thought, why not? I went with all my stress about my identity, all my questions about why I was born, why I was here.

"There were Bible studies and revival meetings and sermons at this camp run by Mennonites. I don't remember what they covered, but I do remember one verse—Matthew 6:33: 'Strive first for the kingdom of God and his righteousness, and all these things will be given to you as well.'

"That suddenly became my answer. It focused my thinking so much that I went forward at the altar call. I surprised my friend!

"Then he asked me through my tears, 'Do you want to go to seminary?' I said, 'Seminary—what is that?' He said, 'To become a *pendeta*' (a Hindu word for *pastor*). I said yes. But now I needed to ask my father, who would have to pay for this instead of medical school.

"To my surprise, he said yes. But he added some advice: 'Don't retreat. Whatever you start, keep going.'"

It may have been a miraculous sort of entrée to the Christian world and way of doing things, but some hurdles lay ahead. Two weeks later, Mesach's friend took him to the seminary to apply for admission. "I saw the prerequisites—I had to be baptized and to have related to a church for two years—and I saw I was disqualified. But I decided to take up my verse, Matthew 6:33. I applied anyway.

"Then I had to be interviewed. It was my first direct experience with a white man. He looked at me with those eyes. I didn't know how to answer his questions about my church membership. Finally I asked him, 'Am I accepted?' 'Well,' he said, 'I'll have to consult with my team.'

"Within a month I got a letter. I opened it with a lot of anxiety. I was the first student to be accepted at this Baptist seminary before being baptized."

To fulfill his course requirements, Mesach on weekends served in a Mennonite church, the Jepara congregation. When he graduated, the congregation invited him to become their full-time pastor.

The setting was Indonesia, but the human dynamics were universal. Mesach recalls his dilemma: "I wasn't sure I wanted to do it. It was my hometown. I knew a lot of people in the church, including some relatives. *But*, I thought, *if they call me . . .*"

The call itself, however, was the subject of controversy within the church. "The congregation was thirty-five years old but had never called a pastor. I was the first person with theological education to be invited; the young people wanted a trained pastor. There was considerable conflict within the church about the whole matter, even on the board."

Two factors finally nudged Mesach to say yes to the invitation. "I appreciated the old pastor; he had provided good leadership for thirty-five years. And my parents were not yet Christians. I wanted them to find faith."

Everything seemed to be in place for Mesach's move into leadership. But the old pastor had one more qualifier: "He said I had to be married before I could be ordained! He had a strict moral code. If I, a single pastor in my midtwenties, visited a single [woman] parishioner, it would raise questions."

Mesach and Miriam met in a church where he had done some weekend practicums. "When we became engaged, she went to seminary for a year to see what this world was like." They were married in the fall of 1965.

A political development left its mark on the newly married couple. In 1967 the Indonesian government decided to clarify the loyalty of its people.

"The government did not believe in dual citizenship, so all Arabs, Chinese, Indians, and others who were residents of Indonesia had to choose their homeland. My family, with Chinese origins—and many others—had been there for four or five generations, but our citizenship was ambiguous. Most of us chose Indonesia.

"Then all of us Chinese were to select names that were Indonesian. It became an opportunity to choose 'Christian' Indonesian names. In our area, the Christians all chose names that incorporated the name 'Christ.' I became 'Mesach Krisetya.' Mesach was one of Daniel's friends in the Old Testament book of Daniel. He was a fireproof man. 'Krisetya' is a two-word term. 'Kris' means 'Christ'; 'Setya' is a Sanskrit word for 'loyal' or 'truthful.' So my names mean 'the fireproof man loyal to Christ.' I hope that I can be one."

Forever identified as a Christian, Mesach has also decided to continue with the Mennonites. "Where I was born anew was with the Mennonites, so I stuck with the Mennonites." Not only has he pastored in Mennonite congregations, he has become a Mennonite professional. Some of his training and internships were done in North American Mennonite institutions.

He has an M.Div. degree from Associated Mennonite Biblical Seminary [AMBS] and a D.Min. from the School of Theology in Claremont, California. He interned at Prairie

View Hospital in Newton, Kansas, and at the Vellore Medical College Hospital in India.

"While in the Baptist seminary in Indonesia, I became quite interested in counseling because I had been helped by that. While I was studying at AMBS in Elkhart, Indiana, a professor told me that he thought practical theology was for me, based on what he knew of me and some testing I did there. So I let New Testament studies go, which I had thought was for me."

The switch in vocational direction seemed to fit Mesach well. Today he is vice president of the International Council on Pastoral Care and Counseling, a professional association, and lectures around the world on issues related to that field. He is on the teaching faculty of Satya Wacana Christian University, where he also heads the Department of Pastoral Care.

Mesach's first brush with Mennonite World Conference (MWC) was in 1972, when he attended the worldwide Assembly in Curitiba, Brazil. C. J. Dyck, then his professor at AMBS, found a sponsor for his trip and sent the fledgling churchman to the international event.

He brought his scalpel-sharp observations to the MWC Executive Committee when he joined it some twenty years later. There he has become a voice for the ever-increasing mutuality among Mennonite fellowships around the world. He is prophetic with a touch of fearlessness.

"Mennonite World Conference is the only organization where Mennonites and Brethren in Christ from around the world can say what they want to say on an equal basis.

"I am still dissatisfied that MWC is seen primarily as an organization that is supposed to arrange the next conference gathering. I want 'communion.' We ought to pick up ideas that create relationships and mutual influence. For example, Joram Mbeba [a Mennonite bishop from Tanzania and fellow MWC Executive Committee member] recently asked me to come to Tanzania to provide some pastoral care and counseling. This is the kind of exchange that can happen with global coordination. Then the world becomes very small.

"Prophetic voices are coming from the Southern Hemisphere, and I believe they will begin to change the church. I believe interdependence will begin to happen, that there will be a new mix. There is a changing mentality in the North. The Northern Hemisphere churches who have had less recent experience in suffering now want to share in our suffering."

Mesach has too little time these days. His own people are under threat as Christians in Indonesia, and he works constantly with other leaders there to address fears and prepare for increasing pressures and unknown dangers. Yet he continues his advocacy for global linkages church-to-church, a growing necessity, he believes.

He isn't imagining a backslapping family reunion among Mennonites. "We will need to decide whether we can agree that we have differences, and that our differences will not separate us. We should not impose our traditions on each other or let doctrine divide us, because doctrine does divide.

"Mennonite World Conference's emphasis should be on service. We do need a common belief and hope, and we have that; then together we serve."

There appears to be nothing so defining for human beings as hard times. Mesach Krisetya became a church leader during political upheaval in his country, and he continues in a church that is under duress. From there he speaks to the global Mennonite fellowship, not as a critic, but as an encourager. His disarming sense of humor and his years of speaking English in North America have prepared him also for a worldwide audience. He addresses it with wisdom and surprising twists on well-known English-language idioms.

Mesach grants that he hasn't learned how to relax, but he can't stop imagining all that could be done, both at home and in churches elsewhere in the world. "I would like to pay more attention to the welfare of the people," he says.

Now Mesach, the fireproof man who is loyal to Christ, is needed both locally and globally. His and Miriam's two sons are raised, he's had the deep satisfaction of seeing his parents become Christians, and he enjoys his work.

The Indonesian churches are leaning on his wisdom and strength in their present danger. Mennonites in many parts of the world are beginning to pay some attention to his prophetic call for a Mennonite world "communion."[65]

Part of a phenomenal history: choir members at a Meserete Kristos Church, Addis Ababa, Ethiopia.

INSET Bedru Hussein, Ethiopian leader and vice president of Mennonite World Conference.

Through the Eye of a Needle

Merle Good

Eastern Mennonite Missions (EMM) planted the
Mennonite Church in Ethiopia in 1948. During an
administrative visit, EMM executive Paul Kraybill partic-
ipated in the baptism of a new believer. After he had
received the water of baptism, the Ethiopian believer
made a request: "I have accepted your God and joined
your church; now tell me your history." Kraybill
answered, "You don't want to know our history. It's a
bad history." The Ethiopian responded with uncharac-
teristic wisdom: "Bad history is better than no history."[66]
The Mennonite Church in Ethiopia—the Meserete
Kristos Church—now has a phenomenal history. For ten
years it was forced underground by a Marxist govern-
ment. During that decade its membership exploded,
multiplying ten times. Bedru Hussein was a part of
that growth.

A SEVENTH-GRADE Ethiopian boy was playing with his
friends during recess when the wind blew several pieces
of paper across the schoolyard. Young Bedru was drawn to
one that carried English words.

He took the paper in to his teacher and asked what it
meant. The teacher in the government school wrote the

words on the board, but no one understood them: "It is easier for a camel to go through the eye of a needle than for someone who is rich to enter the kingdom of God."

No one could explain it. Then an elderly man who had come to school late in life raised his hand and said it was from the New Testament (Mark 10:25). He explained about the gates surrounding Jerusalem, with one called Eye of the Needle. He told the class how a merchant, to enter the city, had to unload the camel, stoop down, drag the goods to the other side, then pull the camel through, and finally remount.

"That stayed in my heart a long time," Bedru remembers. The old man told the class about Jesus and his practice of illustrating spiritual realities with physical examples. It was a vivid experience.

In 1990-92 Bedru Hussein served as Acting Executive Secretary of the Meserete Kristos Church (MKC), the Mennonite Church in Ethiopia; then he was Executive Secretary of MKC from 1992 to 1997, when he left to study at Eastern Mennonite Seminary for three years. From 1997 Bedru has served as vice president of Mennonite World Conference. Beginning in July 2000, he is Associate Principal of Meserete Kristos College. He has come a long distance from his Muslim childhood.

Bedru was the first in his family to become a Christian. His decision brought opposition and difficulty. "One day I saw a friend in the cafeteria at school with an unusually bright face," he remembers. "I was in grade twelve and had a great spiritual hunger, but there was no one to teach me."

Bedru's friend was a Pentecostal Christian who invited him to a youth center in Addis Ababa, to see a film. He felt drawn in by the event. "Tears were flowing down my face, and I accepted Jesus as my Savior that night."

These new friends told him about the baptism of the Holy Spirit. "I said, 'If God gives it to me, why not?' So the next evening at dusk, we went to an empty football field and started to pray (there were five or six of us). As soon as we started praying, I got filled! It was a glorious experience for me."

Everything changed for Bedru. "I started to love people—that was a change. And I knew Christ was in me."

His father opposed him. "He would not talk with me or eat with me for three solid months. He was very angry. He said I may have to leave the house."

Bedru's mother gradually listened to his testimony and started to believe. Bedru's brothers and sisters began to attend his church, also. His father was in the military and had to go on assignment for six months. Bedru wrote to him to explain his new faith. At one point his father replied, "Pray for me, that I may come to the light."

Bedru hoped to become a doctor. While studying biology at the university, he also sang in the choir of the Pentecostal church begun by the students. He started to preach and witness, and people responded to his ministry.

Years later, after he had learned to know the Mennonites and when the Mennonite church had to go underground, he looked back on these student days as times of great instruction. His first imprisonment came in 1972, when an informer infiltrated their group. The military police came to their place of worship; twenty-one were arrested and put in prison. Three of them were placed in a special cell, where the police beat them.

"I felt like I was beaten by a sponge. It was the grace of God—I remember it very clearly." The beating was severe, but Bedru suffered no bleeding or broken bones.

Later they were put on trial for illegal assembly, charged a small fine, and released with the warning not to meet again. But after a month, they resumed underground meetings, early in the morning or late at night, for four years.

Months later he and his wife were both imprisoned, along with two hundred others, when they attended church in Addis Ababa. After two weeks in prison, they were released on bail and required to report to the court monthly.

There were to be no more church meetings or they would automatically go to jail for two years without trial. Bedru believes the Orthodox Church encouraged the military police in its policies.

By now Bedru was a high school biology teacher, but he was also learning that he enjoyed being a Bible teacher. In 1976 he moved with his family to Nazareth, Ethiopia, where he would teach at the Nazareth Bible Academy operated by Mennonites. "I knew Mennonites in university, but this was my first association with them."

Over time Bedru became an elder and started to work with the leadership of the Meserete Kristos Church, which had about 3,000 members at the time. He joined the MKC Executive Committee and helped with leadership training for Mennonites as well as other denominational leaders.

"The revival grew at the same time that the Communist movement was growing," he recalls in a voice at once gentle and intense. Tension and struggle characterized these years, "but the groundwork for the later underground church was being laid."

Then in 1982, the church and the school were nationalized. Six prominent Mennonite leaders were imprisoned. The money in the bank was frozen. Bedru became director of the Nazareth school for the balance of the year; then it became a Marxist school. "We had to hand everything over to the government. Meserete Kristos Church seemed especially targeted because it was attracting so many young people."

Bedru moved to the capital city with his wife, Kelemwork Belete, three sons, and one daughter; he joined a health research institute. There he became deeply involved with the underground church. "I felt a stronger and stronger call. I could not resist it. I became a full-time minister in 1990."

The institute issued an attractive offer to Bedru to go to Michigan State University for his master's degree. "What should I do? I told my wife that if God and the church call me, I will serve the church and not go to the States."

That's when Bedru was called to become Executive Secretary of the Mennonite Church in Ethiopia. In May 1992, the Marxist government fell. As the church resurfaced, they discovered that they had grown from five thousand members before they were forced underground to fifty thousand—ten times as many! Their current membership is more than a hundred thousand strong and has spread from two regions to all parts of the country. A remarkable story, to say the least.

The growth in the Mennonite church in Ethiopia has been unusual, but other evangelical groups are growing too. So are the Muslims, as people leave the Coptic Church.

To prepare for his leadership roles, Bedru came to the United States to study at Eastern Mennonite Seminary. He has now returned to Ethiopia, where leadership training has become one of his top priorities for the church. His Muslim roots continue to underlie his concern that Ethiopia may become an Islamic state as the Muslims gain ground. Yet his faith is secure in a future buoyed by the grace of God. He knows it is possible for a camel to go through the eye of a needle.[67]

First Hispanic Mennonite pastor, David Castillo, begins a mission in La Junta, Colorado, by gathering children for Sunday school, 1940.

INSET Dynamic and congenial: Samuel Lopez with Felipe Cantu and Juanita F. Nunez.

Samuel's Story

Richard Showalter

*Nine Mexican immigrants were baptized in Chicago on
Sunday, April 29, 1934. Since then, Spanish has been one
of the worship languages of North American
Mennonites. That baptism at the Chicago Home Mission
marks the founding of the first Hispanic Mennonite congregation. David Castillo, also a Mexican immigrant,
was the first pastor.[68] Since the mustard-seed beginning,
Spanish-speaking congregations have grown faster than
any other North American Mennonite group. Current
membership is over 3,500. Samuel Lopez contributes to
this growth in his ministry as pastor, church planter, and
president of the Hispanic Mennonite Convention of
Churches in the United States
and Canada.*

ACTUALLY, IT'S NOT a story, but stories. And it's not
Samuel's story; it's God's story.

A quiet, unobtrusive, much-loved man, Samuel Lopez
walks among us as a bridge builder, with a radiance born of
the assurances of the presence of God. A Mexican by birth,
he has served for a decade as president of the Hispanic
Mennonite Convention of Churches in the USA and Canada.
He leads the Spanish Council of Lancaster Conference,
serves as an overseer, and has been a pastor and an Eastern
Mennonite Missions (EMM) Executive Committee member.

Samuel grew up in Mexico, supported by parents who worked in the U.S. and sent enough money to the children to meet their needs. The oldest, Samuel sometimes rented a house for all of them. At other times, they lived with relatives. He knew nothing of Christianity except that his grandfather named him Samuel and taught him a few Bible verses.

When he was seventeen, his parents sent to Mexico for their children, and Samuel reluctantly obeyed. But on arrival in the U.S., he learned that their father and mother had separated, forcing the children to choose between them. In the ensuing crisis, Samuel's aunt invited him to a little Hispanic Mennonite church in Chicago. Four days later, he knelt at home and asked Jesus to be his Lord and Savior.

His life was never the same. Within three weeks he was baptized. Shortly afterward, in a Sunday service, he and a couple other Hispanic youth volunteered to attend a Nazarene Bible college in Texas. To Samuel's surprise, his father, who thought he was crazy for going to Bible college, called an hour before he left and said, "Go in peace."

When asked at seminary what his vocational goal was, he said, "I don't know. I just want to study the Bible." When asked what a Mennonite is, he said again, "I don't know."

It was a foreign world, and the first semester he made D's. But after crying out to God for help, he made A's the next semester and went on to complete four years' work in three. One time, Mennonite historian and theologian J. C. Wenger of Associated Mennonite Biblical Seminary (AMBS), Elkhart, Indiana, stopped in to visit. Samuel observed that unlike other important people, J. C. didn't stay aloof, but loved all the students, mingling with them freely. "That's when I understood what a Mennonite is," Samuel said. "He witnessed beyond words."

Samuel's life has been a patchwork of responses to Jesus, responses that many around him thought "crazy" or "dumb." He later graduated from Goshen (IN) College and AMBS. When he left AMBS, he was expected to become a pastor. But lacking peace from God, he went to Oregon and worked as a migrant, swinging a machete among his fellow Mexicans. While there, he sensed God calling him to Pennsylvania, an unknown place.

He set out with his young family and arrived in Lancaster County with $10. For some weeks they stayed in the New Holland Spanish Mennonite meetinghouse, telling no one about his credentials, but doing what he was asked. At first, some thought him irresponsible; yet after three months, he was invited to become their pastor.

Samuel is also unassuming as a church planter and evangelist. With uncommon clarity about God's leading, he walks into a new setting and soon establishes a new witness. When a pastor is in place, Samuel serves as overseer in a way that empowers and affirms the pastor's calling.

Where might one find Samuel today? Likely somewhere hanging out with children! He never forgot J. C. Wenger's testimony of presence, showing what a true disciple is. Kingdom sense is not "common sense."[69]

Ushering in the new: Moderators Ron Sawatsky (Mennonite Church Canada) and Lee Snyder (Mennonite Church USA) are commissioned at St. Louis 99. Their pastors, Sue Clemmer (left) and Dorothy Nickel Friesen, offered the commissioning prayers.

INSET Elfrieda and Peter Dyck pointed the way to integration.

Drinking Anabaptist Tea and Other Tales of Integration

Peter J. Dyck

The road to integration has been a long one. Herald of
Truth *editor John F. Funk, who helped Russian
Mennonites migrate to the prairie states and provinces in
the 1870s, hoped the immigrants would join MC conferences. They didn't. MCs and GCs cooperated in sending
relief supplies to India during the great famine of 1896-
97. When sending food and money led to sending missionaries to India, GC leaders asked MC leaders whether
they could cooperate. MCs said no. Mennonite Central
Committee, however, was inter-Mennonite from its
beginning in 1920. MCs and GCs worked and prayed
together during Civilian Public Service (CPS), 1941-46.
Goshen Biblical Seminary (MC) and Mennonite Biblical
Seminary (GC) affiliated to become Associated
Mennonite Biblical Seminary. Such shared experiences
led to the formation of dually affiliated congregations—
129 by 1995. Peter and Elfrieda Dyck know about this
journey from personal experience, as the following
vignettes illustrate.*

Scene One

ELFRIEDA AND I had been serving with the Mennonite Central Committee (MCC) in Europe for almost ten years when we met with the Executive Committee in the old Atlantic Hotel in Chicago. The year was 1949, and we were terminating our MCC service, at least for the time being, to finish my college education. During a break, Rev. J. J. Thiessen, a great leader and wonderful Christian, the man who had ordained me a few years earlier, took me aside for a serious discussion. "Is it true," he wanted to know, "that you are going to attend Goshen College?"

I told him that what he had heard was true. I also shared with him that the major reason for this was to hear Harold Bender lecture on Anabaptism. Thiessen was not pleased. He tried to dissuade me, giving one reason after another why Goshen was not a good choice. "Why not go to Bethel College, or Bluffton College?" I will always remember his final comment, given in all seriousness: "As a General Conference member, not a teenager but already thirty-four years old, you are setting a bad example for the youth of the General Conference."

Scene Two

We went to Goshen. We had barely unpacked our suitcases and registered when I was called into the office of the president. Ernest Miller welcomed me warmly, chatted about this and that, and finally came to the point. "You are older than most students," he began. "You have served many years with MCC. You are ordained. You and Elfrieda have gained visibility in our churches from reporting on the refugee movement."

He paused, and I had no idea what he was leading up to. Finally he asked, "Because of all this, do you expect to receive some financial consideration from Goshen College? A discount perhaps, or a scholarship?"

We had no money, and the idea of a discount sounded

good to me. It would mean needing to borrow less. However, had I expected it? My answer was no. Miller was visibly relieved. He proceeded to explain that the college could not give me financial aid since I didn't belong to the "Old" Mennonite Church. Giving me aid could be interpreted by the General Conference Mennonites as wooing one of their members away from them.

Scene Three
Around 1952, Harold S. Bender and I were visiting in his living room. He asked whether my brother C. J., who was then serving with MCC in South America, was also going to attend Goshen College as I had done. Jokingly, I said, "It's enough for one in the family to make that mistake!" Then more seriously I talked of my good experiences and said that I coveted the same for many of our General Conference young people.

We continued the discussion about GC-MC cooperation in education, especially on the seminary level. Finally we agreed to invite some brothers, no more than four from each of the two conferences, for an informal discussion. I was to invite the GC representatives and Bender was to invite the MC people. I remember his suggestion that we meet in his home and that Elizabeth would serve tea. "Nobody can fault us for getting together and drinking Anabaptist tea," he said.

The meeting did take place. Brother Bender asked me to introduce the subject. That took me by surprise, but I began by sharing about my own good experience as a General Conference student at Goshen College and Seminary. I said I hoped we might explore ways of moving closer together in our separate programs. By that time, I was attending the GC and Church of the Brethren Seminary in Chicago.

There were some questions, a few concerns, and one or two cautious but positive statements. I was disappointed. I guess I had expected too much from this meeting. Orie Miller was the first to leave, after saying little. As he left, he simply said, "Thanks for the tea." For some time afterward, I referred to that gathering as the thanks-for-the-tea meeting.

Nevertheless, the ball had started to roll. More informal meetings followed. More people participated. Usually they were in connection with other meetings, such as the MCC annual meeting in the Atlantic Hotel in Chicago.

Then one day the conversations became official, and minutes were kept. The rest, as they say, is history.

Scene Four

In 1967 MCC transferred us from Europe, where we had been serving for another decade, to Akron, Pennsylvania. After attending the Akron Mennonite Church (MC) for a while, we decided to become members. We wanted dual membership, but that turned out to be more difficult than we had anticipated. First the pastor and then a committee told us that we couldn't have dual membership. We suggested that perhaps the time had come for the entire congregation to belong to both the MC and GC conferences. That fell on deaf ears.

Ultimately they relented and said we could have our primary membership in the Akron congregation and a secondary membership in the General Conference Mennonite Eden congregation of Moundridge, Kansas. We objected. We asked for equal and full membership in both denominations. In later discussions, members asked us, "If you belong to both the GC and MC conferences, would you subscribe to both *The Mennonite* and the *Gospel Herald*? Are you going to double or halve your giving? Will you attend both the MC and GC general assemblies?"

Statistics was a final argument intended to persuade us of the folly of dual membership: "Suppose we all became dual members. Just look how that would mess up our membership statistics. Overnight we would have doubled, because we would all be counted twice, once by the GCs and again by the MCs." Someone suggested that the trouble with

Elflrieda and me was that we had been too long in MCC. But then it happened, praise the Lord!

A few years later the Akron church voted unanimously to become a dual-conference church. We did subscribe to *The Mennonite* and the *Gospel Herald*. We did attend both assemblies. The church did, and still does, contribute financially to both MC and GC mission boards, colleges, and other agencies.

It was a bit of a hassle. On the surface, it didn't make much sense. But we did it because everybody believed that this was a temporary inconvenience on the road to full amalgamation. Basic to all of this was the desire to strengthen our witness in the world, to heed the prayer of Jesus "that they may all be one, . . . so that the world may believe that you have sent me" (John 17:21).

Scene Five
Then came the Bethlehem 83 assembly, where GC moderator Jake Tilitzky and MC moderator Ross Bender stood to welcome delegates. Two podiums had been placed at opposite ends of the stage. The moderators picked up the podiums and moved slowly toward each other, dialoguing as they went. Finally they met in the middle, shook hands, and embraced.

The applause was overwhelming! What began as a simple pragmatic procedure became a prophetic, symbolic move. We were all ready to become *one* conference. God was breathing a new Spirit into our churches.

Scene Six
Other joint assemblies came and resolutions were passed. Wichita 95 delegates said, "Let's do it." Winnipeg and Orlando 97 assemblies chose a name and a periodical. At St. Louis 99 fifteen resolutions were passed, but we balked on the membership question and fell apart at the forty-ninth parallel. Suddenly the border between Canada and the

United States loomed large on the horizon. It had become a major issue in General Board meetings, and some said: "Our agenda is different! You don't understand us! We need our own conferences, one in Canada and one in the United States." But is that what the people really wanted?

Sometimes the agenda will be different, but that doesn't have to divide us. The divisive spirit so characteristic in our society, and in the world, has influenced and shaped our Mennonite thinking. I believe the angels in heaven are not the only ones weeping.

Tim Kennel, Peter Eash Scott, Katherine Lemons, and Sidney King tracing Kratz's trail at Chortitza, Russia.

INSET Clayton Kratz: still touching lives and compelling people to action.

In the Footsteps of
Clayton Kratz

Sidney King

THE *disappearance of Clayton Kratz (1896-1920) in
Russia shocked his contemporaries and intrigued successive generations. Kratz, a Goshen College student and
native of Blooming Glen, Pennsylvania, joined Arthur
Slagel (1891-1943) and Orie O. Miller (1892-1977) in
delivering humanitarian aid to Ukrainian Mennonites in
the aftermath of World War I. Lingering intrigue surrounding his mysterious disappearance compelled four
twenty-somethings—Sidney King, Katherine Lemons,
Tim Kennel, and Peter Eash Scott—in July of 2000 to
follow Kratz's trail to Greece, Turkey, and the Ukraine.
They hoped to unearth clues for solving the mystery surrounding Kratz's arrest and probable execution. In the
process they ask probing questions about faith, martyrdom, and their own generation's relationship to the
church in a postmodern era. The four have produced a
video documenting their journey and their questions.*

FOR THREE YOUNG Mennonites in 1920, it was undoubtedly a fantastic adventure: they were on their way to administer relief supplies to the war- and famine-stricken Russian
Mennonites. Arthur Slagel, Orie Miller, and Clayton Kratz
traveled from New York to Athens to the interior of Russia

by boat, train, motorcycle, and carriage. Along the way they experienced new worlds of beauty, strangeness, extravagance, and ultimately, danger. Their journey took them from the art museums of Italy to a meeting with the pope, and on to the teeming streets of Constantinople. The experience left none of them unchanged.

Eighty years later and under quite different circumstances, the four of us were also on a journey of discovery. Along the way, we stood at the gleaming stones of the Acropolis, heard a hundred-year-old Russian Mennonite woman describe firsthand the horrors of the famine and Nestor Machno's reign of terror, and crossed the moonlit Black Sea on the *Caledonia*. On one level it was journey of immediate and experiential discovery; on another level the sights and sounds we encountered also led us to new levels of discovery in the story of Clayton Kratz.

The basic elements of the story are familiar. Clayton Kratz was a rising senior at Goshen College, popular, talented, full of promise, and engaged to be married. He left on the brink of his final year of college to accept the call of the fledging Mennonite Central Committee to administer relief to Russian Mennonites suffering from civil war and famine.

Clayton was the third man chosen to accompany two already selected, Arthur Slagel and Orie Miller. Slagel, of Flanagan, Illinois, was a young professor at Hesston College with remarkable linguistic skills and eager to make a contribution in the area of active nonviolence and service. At the age of twenty-eight, Miller, of Akron, Pennsylvania, was already making a name for himself as a young church leader, with overseas experience in the Near East relief effort.

Two months into the trip, Kratz disappeared, leaving only a scant paper trail and many unanswered questions in his wake. Through the haze of history, it is difficult to get a firm grasp on the personal face of Kratz; it is much easier to treat him as an icon or archetype, but to do this betrays the depth of the story.

Born in 1896 near Blooming Glen in Bucks County, Pennsylvania, the sixth child of Elizabeth and William Kratz, Clayton was, by all accounts, a well-behaved and well-liked boy who exuded promise. He was the first in his family to attend college, enrolling at Goshen College after teaching school. His list of academic and extracurricular accomplishments at Goshen is enough to make any parent proud: member of the baseball team, prize-winning orator, president of the junior class—the list seems endless. He was even elected "best-looking" by his classmates. Pictures from the time show a confident young man, at times properly dressed and looking serious, at other times clearly at ease and enjoying himself with friends.

The contrast between Kratz's almost charmed life at Goshen and his final days in Russia is almost too large to fathom. This contrast is one aspect of the story that makes it so compelling. What road took Kratz from his world as a popular and gifted student to being arrested and beaten, and then disappearing in the freezing predawn cold of a war-torn Russia?

That road began when Kratz received a telegram from the MCC office, asking him to be the third man to join Miller and Slagel on the trip to Russia. Kratz was given two days to respond, but he needed less than one. He was willing to postpone his academic career and leave behind all he knew to enter a world of which he knew virtually nothing, only that he was needed.

It is difficult to imagine the full breadth of experiences and responses he must have had along the way. He and his companions left precious little that sheds light on their personal feelings and responses to what they were seeing and experiencing. In this time when talk shows clog the airways and tell-all memoirs are best-sellers, it is hard for us to relate to an age when full disclosure wasn't valued as highly as discretion. Yet this reality is evident in reading the journals and letters left by the three men: they tend to be fact-oriented, long on descriptions of buildings and travel times, and short on reflection.

In a way this is a mixed blessing. On one hand it would be wonderful to know about everything from the interpersonal dynamics among the three to what they missed most about home. On the other hand, the lack of such confessional or revelatory records leave enough questions unanswered so that readers and video viewers can search out their own answers to the questions. Thus the story becomes more personal and meaningful. Regardless of how we raise and answer these questions, we find it easy to admire the serious-minded and resolute way the three young men went about their work.

Clayton Kratz's name may not be as familiar to Mennonites today as H. S. Bender or Orie O. Miller. Many Goshen College students live in the dormitory bearing his name without knowing anything about him. However, Kratz is not yet in danger of disappearing into oblivion. The Clayton Kratz Fellowship in eastern Pennsylvania, a student dormitory on the campus of Goshen College, a work of fiction by Geraldine Gross Harder, a video by John L. Ruth, and an active oral history—these all ensure that Kratz's story will be told, retold, and remembered.

Nevertheless, there is a danger in letting history and stories, especially important ones, grow too familiar. The beauty and complexity of what is closest and most familiar is often easiest to overlook. The Kratz story is certainly engaging on an immediate level, but it is also a more complicated story than commonly recognized. One of our great pleasures in working on the video was exploring the many facets of the story; peeling away one layer revealed another, that upon inspection changed the way we viewed previous layers.

Everyone wonders what happened to Kratz. But there are other telling questions that also need to be considered, questions that inject a very human element into the story.

How did Kratz's relationship with his brother Jacob, who

enrolled in the military during World War I, affect his decision to go to Russia? What did Istanbul look like through the eyes of a twenty-four-year old Mennonite from Bucks County, Pennsylvania? How did Kratz feel while crossing the Black Sea on the American destroyer *Whipple*, ducking beneath the massive guns on deck and sharing sleeping quarters with navy officers? How did he occupy his time during his final days in Halbstadt (in Molotschna settlement, South Russia)?

History is not recorded in a vacuum, and stories are not passed to successive generations without undergoing processes of transformation and adaptation. They must be reborn and retold if they are to survive. Particularly in a faith tradition that has valued martyrdom and suffering, our generation of Mennonites is at a crossroads in interpreting that history.

Postmodernism has found a toehold in the current generation of Mennonite students, and the postmodern lens is not a particularly kind judge of the value of martyrdom. What is martyrdom other than the willingness to lay down one's life out of a belief in an absolute Truth? Is it possible to celebrate and affirm the value of such a decision without holding the exact beliefs? Is a complete adjustment of the definition of martyrdom necessary?

These questions and an intense desire to secure a more complete and human understanding of the story attracted the four of us to take a trip across the ocean, seeking out and following the trail of the three young men. But no matter how personally enthused and engaged the four of us were with the subject matter, we still had to face two questions: Why in the summer of 2000 was a new video based on the life and travels of Clayton Kratz needed? Were we capable of producing it?

On an immediate level, the recent surfacing of C. E. Krehbiel's diary merits a new look at the Kratz story. Krehbiel was an MCC worker in Russia in 1922-23 who made inquiries into Kratz's disappearance during his service there. Other MCC workers, perhaps most notably A. J. Miller, also did some investigating and made appeals to the Russian government for any information on Kratz. Their efforts brought no answers to the persisting questions and speculation.

In fact, subsequent efforts by MCC workers and officials to determine Kratz's fate were fruitless. Speculation on the disposition of Kratz's case ranged widely: perhaps he was executed or died of typhus or was working in coal mines in Siberia. One Russian official even claimed that Kratz had been placed on a train for Norway, where he was to be released from Russian custody.

After eighty years of virtually no information or discoveries, the Krehbiel diary offers answers. It provides a cause of death, means of execution, charges leveled against Kratz, a villain, and a motive. There is even a reference to a numbered document that may be suffocating somewhere beneath eighty years of Soviet bureaucracy.

August 15, 1922

A Mrs. Dyck called this afternoon and said she knew the man who [killed] Kratz. His alias at present is Grigori Saposhnikov. He has lived in her house for 11 months and wants to go to the U.S. He runs an electric plant. He is a Jew and has a wife and no children. He is supposed to be a bad man in general.

December 24, 1922

Johann Wall made inquiry at Kharkow on Clayton Kratz, and through a Jew he knows from Lodz, found that records of Kharkow (3853a) state that Kratz was arrested at Halbstadt by Bagon, etc., the latter having accused him or charged [him] with being an English spy of the government, and that he was then brought to Bachmut, etc., and finally to

Kharkow, where he was turned over the Gubernia at Alexandrowsk, and the records says [he was] shot there!

Promising, yes. Tantalizing, certainly. But at the same time, the Krehbiel diary essentially boils down to hearsay. Krehbiel himself did not see document 3538a in Kharkow and did not talk to Grigori Saposhnikov. Yet however reliable or unreliable Krehbiehl's sources may have been, and even if his reports are accepted at face value, new questions arise to take the place of the old.

With so many people back home starving for any piece of news, the question of why Krehbiel kept his findings secret is a mystery nearly as engaging as Kratz's disappearance. It is tempting to speculate: Perhaps Krehbiel dreaded the thought of shattering any remaining hopes in the Kratz family or his fiancée, Edith Miller. Perhaps he realized the secondhand nature of the information and didn't want to assume personal responsibility for it or its consequences. Perhaps Krehbiel viewed the reference to Saposhnikov, a Jew, as information too inflammatory to justify making a report.

Nevertheless, to become too consumed with the details and tantalizing fragments of the diary is to miss the point. As exciting as the Krehbiel diary is, to one inclined to believe everything in it, there are no seismic changes to what had already been assumed. To a skeptic, it raises more questions than it answers. So while the Krehbiel diary is certainly a significant development, and was for our group somewhat of a catalyst for making the video, it is still only a part of the total picture.

When the idea of making a video about Kratz was still more idea than reality, we talked to Professor John D. Roth, who encouraged and supported our idea and enthusiasm, but was sure to articulate some of the challenges ahead. For instance, the fact that John L. Ruth had already made a video about Kratz would raise questions of pertinence in the minds of many viewers and supporters. Roth also advised us to prepare ourselves to answer the question of what authority we had to present this story. This question certainly tempered our enthusiasm. But as we resolved to go forward with the project, we found that the answer lay in the story itself.

Both Miller and Slagel were still in their twenties at the time of the trip, and Kratz was twenty-four with another year of school ahead of him. It is hard to overstate the importance and risk of their work. They were granted leadership in the groundbreaking steps of forging Mennonite Central Committee. They were assigned a task of organizing and delivering tons of relief supplies into the interior of a war-ravaged country. To do this, they had to chart unfamiliar territory and navigate through nightmarish bureaucracies, formidable tasks now, much more so in 1920.

It is difficult for us to imagine that the church of today would select a team of three twenty-somethings to fill a role of such importance. One may wonder whether that has more to do with the church or the young people. Nevertheless, the bottom line is that leadership positions in the church and church-affiliated organizations simply aren't available for young people to the extent they were in 1920, or even in 1960.

These three young men shouldered heavy responsibility and delivered results under great pressures and stresses Their example is inspiring and shows the potential impact that young people can have on the church.

The elements of mystery, intrigue, and war make gripping this 1920 story of the three service pioneers. Their faith, dedication, courage, and unfaltering belief in the justness of their cause pierces the layers of history shrouding the story, bringing it to life for us four young people on the brink of life-changing choices.

We may differ on our perception of the story and what we take away from it. Yet one thing all four of us feel strongly about and see manifest in this story is that young people of the church have a voice; they can be capable producers and leaders when given the opportunity and support.

The story of Clayton Kratz is still touching lives and compelling people to action. We hope our video will, at least in a small way, continue this process.

Photo Credits

AMC = Archives of the Mennonite Church, Goshen, Ind.
MLA = Mennonite Library and Archives, Bethel College, North
  Newton, Kan.

Amish or Shawnee? The Hochstetlers of Northkill
  Tom Lions: This oil painting, *Tom Lions*, depicts the artist's and
    Loren Wengerd's concept of a scene from the Hochstetler
    Massacre of 1757. The artist is Sam B. McCausland of
    Cincinnati, Ohio. The painting was commissioned by Loren
    Wengerd, a ninth-generation descendant of Jacob Hochstetler.
    Sam McCausland is an expert on the types of weapons, dress,
    and lifestyles of the eastern woodland Indians in the 1700s. He
    also has done research on the type of cabins built by wilderness
    settlers. Color prints, signed and numbered 1 to 1,000, were
    printed in 1996. Many of these prints have already been pur-
    chased by descendants and collectors from Florida to California
    and even as far away as Italy. Included with each print will be a
    copy of "Account of the 1757 Hochstetler Massacre," suitable
    for framing; and a certificate of authenticity, a type of docu-
    ment assuring the buyer that these prints will never be repro-
    duced. The prints sell for $145. Remarques are available on
    each print for an additional charge of $50. These highly collec-
    table prints are on the best quality 80# Karma acid-free paper.
    For more information and to order a print, write or telephone:
    Loren and Ruth Wengerd, 0146 U.S. 62, Wilmot, OH 44689,
    Phone 330-359-5151.
  Marker: Daniel E. Hochstetler, Goshen, Ind.
A Cheyenne Legacy at the Washita River
  Battle scene: Library of Congress.
  Hart portrait: John E. Sharp, AMC.
Keeping House as We Understand It
  Meetinghouse: John L. Ruth, Harleysville, Pa.
  Fraktur: American bicentennial fraktur by Roma Jacobs Ruth,
    Harleysville, Pa., 1975.
Escaping the Confederacy
  Wagon: National Archives, Civil War, list no. 13.
  Brunk portrait: South Central Mennonite Conference Photograph
    Album, AMC.

David Goerz, Russian Mennonite Pioneer
Bethel College: MLA.
Goerz portrait: MLA.

Father Stuckey and the Central Conference
Conference gathering: Bluffton College Archives, Bluffton, Ohio.
Stuckey portrait: Bluffton College Archives, Bluffton, Ohio.

David and the Promised Land
Schellenberg family: Arthur Slagel, MCC Collection, AMC.
Toews portrait: MLA.

The Cherokee Run
Wagon: "The Covered Wagon of the Great Western Migration,
    1886," National Archives, American West, list no. 134.
Camp: Photo by C. P. Rich, "Holding Down a Lot in Guthrie,"
    ca. 1889, National Archives, American West, list no. 136.

Annie, the *Titanic,* and a School in India
School group: MLA.
Funk portrait: MLA.

Showdown in Burrton, Kansas
Schrag family: MLA.
Political cartoon: From *New York Evening Telegram,* reprinted in
    Outlook, Jan. 5, 1916, 8, and in *Mennonite Life,* Sept. 1975, 13.

Revolution in Russia
Armed group: MLA.
Nestor Makhno: Museum of the Revolution, Moscow.

The Bishops and the Nightingale
Couple with radio: John Harshbarger Collection, AMC.
Leed portrait: Reprinted by permission from *Festival Quarterly.*

A Soft Voice Speaking Truth Saves the Day
General Conference meeting: Mennonite General Conference
    Collection, AMC.
Yoder and Yoder: S. C. Yoder Photograph Collection, AMC.

A Mennonite Imposter
Ship: MLA.
Joop family: Peter J. and Elfrieda Dyck.

Escape from Communism
New home amid ruins: MLA.
Refugees: Karl Goetz, MLA.

Doing Good in Wartime
Hospital sign: MCC Collection, AMC.
CPSer serving a man: MCC Collection, AMC.

Presenting the Anabaptist Vision
Speech notes: Harold S. Bender Collection, AMC.
Bender portrait: Harold S. Bender Collection, AMC.

Revive Us Again: Brunk Brothers Tent Revivals
Tent meeting: Theron F. Schlabach Photograph Collection, AMC.
Brunk brothers: George R. Brunk II, Harrisonburg, Va.

Out of the Storm Clouds
> *MDS:* MDS Kansas, in *The Hammer Rings Hope* (Herald Press, 2000), by Lowell Detweiler, 18.
>
> *Flood: Topeka Daily Capitol*, from *Mennonite Life*, Oct. 1956, 173.

French Fries and World Missions
> *Food preparation:* MCC Collection, AMC.
>
> *Miller and Dyck:* Burton Buller, MCC Collection, AMC.

Come Sunday, Will We Be a True Communion?
> *Collage of images:* Thomas Nast, *Emancipation,* Philadelphia: S. Bott, 1865. Wood engraving: Prints and Photographs Division, Library of Congress, Washington, D.C.
>
> *King and Hershberger:* Guy F. Hershberger Collection, AMC.

A Wanderer Comes Home
> *Nurse:* MCC Collection, AMC.
>
> *U.S. troops:* MCC Collection, AMC.

The Threshold Is High
> *Congregation at worship:* Goshen College Public Relations Photograph Collection, AMC.
>
> *Miller and Richards:* Mary E. Klassen, Associated Mennonite Biblical Seminary, Elkhart, Ind., 1998.

A Fireproof Man Loyal to Christ
> *Communion table:* Mennonite World Conference photo, Aug. 1998.
>
> *Krisetya portrait:* Wayne Mark Thomas, Mennonite World Conference photo, 1997.

Through the Eye of a Needle
> *Choir:* Larry Miller, Mennonite World Conference photo, June 1999.
>
> *Hussein portrait:* John E. Sharp, AMC.

Samuel's Story
> *Group:* Mennonite Home Mission, Chicago Collection, AMC.
>
> *Trio:* John E. Sharp, AMC.

Drinking Anabaptist Tea and Other Tales of Integration
> *Moderators:* John E. Sharp, AMC.
>
> *Elfrieda and Peter Dyck:* MCC Photograph Collection, AMC.

In the Footsteps of Clayton Kratz
> *Foursome:* Tim Kennel, Goshen College, Goshen, Ind.
>
> *Kratz portrait:* MCC Collection, AMC.

Notes and Story Credits

[1] Quoted by Janeen Bertsche Johnson, "A Future with Hope: Knowing Our Stories," opening sermon, Central District Conference, Mt. Pleasant, Iowa, June 10, 1999, from "Memory in Congregational Life," *Weavings* (Jan./Feb. 1989), 9.

[2] Paul A. W. Wallace, *Indians in Pennsylvania*, 2d ed. (Harrisburg: Pennsylvania Historical and Museum Commission, 1986), 133-7.

[3] Richard K. MacMaster, et. al., *Conscience in Crisis: Mennonites and Other Peace Churches in America, 1739-1789, Interpretation and Documents* (Herald Press, 1979), 126.

[4] Harvey Hostetler, *The Descendants of Jacob Hochstetler, the Immigrant of 1736* (Elgin, Ill.: Brethren Publishing House, 1912), 45.

[5] "Battle of the Washita," General [sic] Custer to General Sheridan, Headquarters, Seventh U.S. Calvary, In the Field of the Washita River, 28 November 1868. Published in *The New York Times*, 30 November 1868 (www.hillsdale.edu/dept/history/documents/war/American Indian/1868-Washita-custer.htm). At the time of this event, Custer was a lieutenant colonel.

[6] Ibid.

[7] Oklahoma state official Website: www.oklaosf.state.ok.us/history.htm.

[8] Originally published as "Legacies of the Massacre and Battle at the Washita," by Lawrence H. Hart, *Oklahoma Today*, May/June, 1999, 58-63.

[9] From John L. Ruth, *Maintaining the Right Fellowship* (Herald Press, 1984), 185-6.

[10] R. J. Heatwole, "A Civil War Story," *Mennonite Historical Bulletin*, Jan. 1948, 3.

[11] Ibid.

[12] Ruth Brunk Stoltzfus, in *Mennonite Women*, ed. Elaine Sommers Rich (Herald Press, 1983), 66.

[13] From *Mennonite Life*, Oct. 1952, 170-5.

[14] Steven R. Estes and Paton Yoder, *Proceedings of the Amish Mennonite Ministers' Meetings, 1862-1878* (Goshen, Ind.: Mennonite Historical Society, 1999), 283-8.

[15] Steven R. Estes, "The Central Conference and the Middle District Merger of 1957," *Mennonite Life* (Mar. 1993), 13.

[16] Harry Yoder, "Joseph Stuckey and Central Conference," *Mennonite Life* (Apr. 1951), 19.

[17] Estes, "The Central Conference," 14.

[18] Janeen Bertsche Johnson, "A Future with Hope: Knowing Our Stories," opening sermon, Central District Conference, Mt. Pleasant, Iowa, June 10, 1999.

[19] From *Mennonite Life,* July 1950; and *Mennonite Historical Bulletin,* Oct. 2000.

[20] From *Mennonite Life,* Oct. 1956, 165-70.

[21] From *Mennonite Life,* Jan. 1957, 44-6.

[22] Peter Schrag, son of John Schrag, interview with author, McPherson Co., Kan., Oct. 23, 1966.

[23] *Der Herold* (published at Newton, Kan.), Nov. 19, 1914; and "Vorwaerts," Nov. 27 and Dec. 13, 1914.

[24] H. P. Krehbiel, "Die Stellung der Gemeinde Jesu Christi zum Modernen Staat," *Der Herold*, Apr. 25, 1918.

[25] Charles Gordon, Hutchinson, Kan., interview with author, Apr. 23, 1967. Gordon was a member of the Burrton mob and confirmed details of this story.

[26] Peter Schrag, interview, Oct. 23, 1966.

[27] *Ibid*. Peter Schrag says his father gave a thousand dollars to the Red Cross and Salvation Army. The Burrton *Graphic* gives the figure of $200 for Nov. 11, 1918.

[28] Burrton *Graphic*, Nov. 14, 1918.

[29] Charles Gordon, interview.

[30] Burrton *Graphic*, Nov. 14, 1918.

[31] Hutchinson *News*, Nov. 16, 1918.

[32] Newton *Evening Kansan-Republican,* quoted in Burrton *Graphic*, Nov. 28, 1918.

[33] Burrton *Graphic*, Dec. 12, 1918.

[34] Newton *Evening Kansan-Republican*, Dec. 27, 1918. See also Wichita *Eagle*, Dec. 27, 1918.

[35] *Ibid*.

[36] *Der Herold*, Jan. 1, 1919.

[37] Gerhard Zerger, interview with author, Moundridge, Kan., Dec. 6, 1966. Fred B. Unruh, interview with author, Burrton, Kan., Jan. 29, 1967. Charles Gordon, interview.

[38] Story from *Mennonite Life*, July 1967, 121-2.

[39] Petr/Peter Arshinov, *History of the Makhnovist Movement, 1918-1921,* trans. Lorraine and Fredy Perlman (Detroit: Black & Red, 1974; London: Freedom Press, 1987), from *Istoriia makhnovskogo dvizheniia.*

[40] From "Nonresistance Tested," *Mennonite Life*, Apr. 1962, 66-8.

[41] From "Doing the Lord's Work: Singing the Lord's Song," *Festival Quarterly*, winter 1986, 23.

[42] From *Edward, Pilgrimage of a Mind: The Journal of Edward Yoder, 1931-1945,* ed. Ida Yoder (Wadsworth, Ohio: Ida Yoder; Irwin, Pa.: Virgil Yoder, c. 1985), xix-xx; and from Allen H. Erb,

Privileged to Serve (Elkhart, Ind.: Mennonite Board of Missions, 1975), 136-43.

[43] From "He Said He Was Heinz Wiebe," *Festival Quarterly*, winter 1987, 11-13; and Peter J. and Elfrieda Dyck, *Up from the Rubble* (Herald Press, 1991), 259-64.

[44] From *Mennonite Life*, Jan. 1951, 6-7.

[45] Since this story was written in 1947, Mennonites have developed various "Mental Health Agencies," as shown in *Mennonite Directory 2001* (Herald Press, 2001), 205-6.

[46] From *Mennonite Life*, Apr. 1947, 8-10, 15. Cf. Alex Sareyan, *The Turning Point: How Persons of Conscience Brought About Major Change in the Care of America's Mentally Ill* (Herald Press, 1994).

[47] Minutes of the Fifty-Fifth Consecutive Meeting of the American Society of Church History, Dec. 28-29, 1943, in *Church History* (Mar. 1944), 56-69.

[48] Information on these events came from correspondence between H. S. Bender and E. R. Hardy Jr., Box 17; Matthew Spinka, Box 22; Thomas C. Pears Jr., Box 11; and Ernst Correll, Box 15; Harold S. Bender Collection, Archives of the Mennonite Church (AMC).

[49] H. S. Bender to E. R. Hardy Jr., Dec. 16, 1943, Box 17, Harold S. Bender Collection, AMC.

[50] Leonard Gross, "Conversations with Elizabeth Bender," *Mennonite Historical Bulletin* (July 1986), 6.

[51] Harold S. Bender, "The Anabaptist Vision," *Church History* 13 (Mar. 1944): 4-24; *The Mennonite Quarterly Review* 18 (Apr. 1944): 67-88; *The Anabaptist Vision* (Herald Press, 1944).

[52] Stanley Shenk journal, entry for Dec. 30, 1991, Goshen, Indiana, AMC.

[53] From Albert Keim's address to the Mennonite Church Historical Association meeting July 29, 1993, in Philadelphia, Pennsylvania, published in the *Mennonite Historical Bulletin*, Oct. 1993. Cf. Albert N. Keim, *Harold S. Bender, 1897-1962* (Herald Press, 1998), 306-31; Guy F. Hershberger, ed., *The Recovery of the Anabaptist Vision: A Sixtieth Anniversary Tribute to Harold S. Bender* (Herald Press, 1957).

[54] From *Mennonite Life*, July 1952, 119, 122-4.

[55] From *Mennonite Life*, Oct. 1956, 172-5, 190. Cf. Katie Funk Wiebe, *Day of Disaster* (Herald Press, 1976); and Lowell Detweiler, *The Hammer Rings Hope: Photos and Stories from Fifty Years of Mennonite Disaster Service* (Herald Press, 2000).

[56] This introduction is by Peter J. Dyck.

[57] From *The Mennonite Encyclopedia 5* (Herald Press, 1990), 588-9.

[58] LeRoy Bechler, *The Black Mennonite Church in North America, 1886-1986* (Herald Press, 1986), 41.

[59] Albert Camus, *De L'envers et l'endroit à L'exil et le royaume* (*From* The right and the wrong side *to* The exile and the kingdom: A retrospective anthology), ed. Germaine Brée (New York: Dell Pub. Co., 1963); as quoted by Alice Walker, *Her Blue Body Everything We Know: Earthling Poems, 1965-1990 Complete* (San Diego: Harcourt Brace Jovanovich, 1991), 6.

[60] Lecture at "A Gathering for Those Seeking to Challenge Racism in the Anabaptist Community," Mar. 4, 1995; first published in "Urban Connections," an inter-Anabaptist urban newsletter; then in *Festival Quarterly,* winter 1996, 19-21.

[61] From "Now I Live in a Setting Where Peacemaking Is the Norm," *Gospel Herald,* Jan. 7, 1997, 6-7.

[62] From *The Mennonite Encyclopedia,* vol. 5 (Herald Press, 1990), 15.

[63] From *Foundation of Christian Doctrine,* in *The Complete Writings of Menno Simons*, trans. L. Verduin, ed. J. C. Wenger (Herald Press, 1956), 161.

[64] From *The Mennonite,* Aug. 4, 1998, 8-9.

[65] "Who Is Mesach Krisetya?" is used by permission from *What Mennonites Are Thinking 1999*, copyright by Good Books; all rights reserved.

[66] From a story told by John L. Ruth, later confirmed by Jean Kraybill.

[67] "Bedru Hussein: Gentle and Intense" first appeared in *Festival Quarterly,* winter 1994; used by permission; all rights reserved.

[68] Rafael Falcón, *The Hispanic Mennonite Church in North America, 1932-1982* (Herald Press, 1986), 33-34.

[69] First published in Eastern Mennonite Missions monthly magazine, *Missionary Messenger*, April 1999.

The Editor

JOHN E. SHARP is director of the Historical Committee and Archives of the Mennonite Church, Goshen, Indiana. Sharp was born near Belleville, in the Kishacoquillas Valley of Pennsylvania, a place full of stories. He attended Rosedale Bible Institute (Irwin, Ohio), Hesston (Kan.) College, Goshen (Ind.) College, and Associated Mennonite Biblical Seminary (Elkhart, Ind.).

For fifteen years Sharp served as a pastor in Kansas and Pennsylvania before beginning his current assignment in 1995. In the Indiana-Michigan Conference, he is an overseer and has served as a congregational mediator. He teaches Sunday school and occasionally preaches at Waterford Mennonite Church, Goshen, where he is a member.

Sharp delights in hearing and telling stories. He is passionate about connecting history and mission, heritage and vision, and counts himself a pastoral historian.

John is married to Michele Miller Sharp, a physician assistant. They have three children, Erin, M. J., and Laura.